From
PAYCHECK
to
POWER

From
PAYCHECK
to
POWER

Linda Bessette &
Anne Owings Wilson

with Helen T. Bennett, Ph.D.

August House Publishers, Inc.
LITTLE ROCK

Printed in the United States of America

10 9 8 7 6 5 4 3 2

LIBRARY OF CONGRESS CATALOGING-IN-PUBLICATION DATA

Bessette, Linda, 1953–
From paycheck to power : the working woman's guide to reducing debt, building assets,
and getting what you want out of life / Linda Bessette and Anne Owings Wilson.
        p.   cm.
ISBN 0-87483-276-4 (hb : alk. paper) : $21.95
ISBN 0-87483-275-6 (pb : alk. paper) : $12.95
1. Women—Finance, Personal.   2. Finance, Personal—Psychological aspects.
I. Wilson, Anne Owings, 1950– .   II. Title.
        HG179.B47   1992
    332.024'042—dc20   92-21864

Executive editor: Liz Parkhurst
Assistant editor: Anne Clancy
Design director: Ted Parkhurst
Cover design: Harvill-Ross Studios, Ltd.
Typography: Lettergraphics / Little Rock

This book is printed on archival-quality paper which meets the
guidelines for performance and durability of the Committee on
Production Guidelines for Book Longevity of the
Council on Library Resources.

AUGUST HOUSE, INC.   PUBLISHERS   LITTLE ROCK

Contents

Acknowledgments

While there are many people to acknowledge and to thank, our appreciation goes first and foremost to those clients who allowed us to share their stories in the writing of this book. The courage of our clients in turning their lives around was the inspiration for writing *From Paycheck to Power*.

Introduction

Money is control. She who has money has control. Control is power. She who has money has power. Control is also safety. She who has money has safety. Money is control and power and safety. She who has the most money has the most control, the most power, and the most safety. All this is *myth*.

Money is a medium of exchange. Money, uncontrolled, can cause you great stress. Money, uncontrolled, can give rise to feelings of powerlessness, insecurity and vulnerability. Controlling money can alleviate stress, can empower you, and can reduce your feelings of helplessness. But no one is ever absolutely in control or absolutely powerful or absolutely safe. All this is *reality*.

We decided to write this book, in large part, to separate myth from reality more clearly. Money is not something to fear or to crave. It is neither the cause of every problem, nor the solution to all your problems. It is only this: a means of exchange. When you control it, you can exchange it for those things that you desire, which are exchangeable for it, whether that is an education, a house, a work of art, food, or time.

When we begin counseling a client on personal money management, we find that within the first thirty days three things happen: (1) The client develops and begins accomplishing a list of tasks to get her money under control; (2) She becomes aware, often for the first time, of the myths under which she has been laboring, usually for many years; and (3) She notices the psychological results of working in a mythical framework.

But let's put it in concrete terms. We discovered two types of clients. One type came to us for useful financial information. Upon receiving that information, this client immediately implemented her plan with little difficulty. The other type came to us for the same useful financial information. But implementing her plan became considerably more difficult. The psychological difficulties surfaced and emotional obstacles came clearly into view. We found that we needed to be aware, and help our clients be aware, of the psychological side of money management.

We also found, time and time again, that those clients who kept reality paramount in their perspective kept their lives in balance and their money in control. Conversely, those clients who kept the myths paramount lacked balance in money matters and in other areas.

This book is intended to do two things, namely, to present a *simple, workable plan* for managing each paycheck, and to identify and deal with the *psychological obstacles* to balanced money management.

The basic money-management plan is simple. You will see "simple" used many times in the text of this book. It is a key word because our financial philosophy is based on simplicity. It is a myth to believe that one cannot manage money well without becoming involved in an array of investment opportunities. The bookstore shelves are filled with books on personal money management that discuss the pros and cons of stocks, bonds, mutual funds, commodities, treasury bills, Ginnie Mae's, annuities ... the list seems endless and increases almost daily as new institutions offer new investment products. These books offer good information to the reader. However, they are based on the supposition that the reader, in fact, has money to invest. The reality is that you can't invest the grocery money, or the money you painstakingly save to send your child to college, or the money you normally use to pay your car insurance. You can only invest money you could afford to lose, and money you do not need to meet your daily obligations.

The reality of everyday life is that most women live from paycheck to paycheck. Most women have very real concerns about where the money will come from that would support them in retirement, pay the current tuition for their children's educations, buy another car when the one in the garage decides to die, or pay that high heating bill in January or the outrageous air conditioning bill in August. For most women, the concept of investing is, and always will be, foreign.

Consequently, our basic money-management plan focuses on exactly what you should do with each paycheck to pay your bills and build your assets.

On the psychological side, we encourage you, throughout the book, to arrive at a new perspective on money—a perspective of balance. Balance will give you freedom of choice. You cannot have absolute control or power or safety, but you can have choice. And, in maintaining your freedom of choice, you maintain the heart of real power: the power to choose. It is both the lack of choice and the inability to choose that make us feel powerless and helpless. Regaining that power is tied directly to functioning within a realistic structure, maintaining balance, and choosing in your own best interest.

As you proceed through the plan, many of you will discover emotional reactions that will hamper your attempts to maintain balance in your money matters. You may be faced with what we call the *seeking-approval* expense, which is an expense incurred to obtain the approval of others, such as your employer, friends, children, or the world at large. Or you may find your money plan sabotaged by an addiction to spending, alcohol, drugs, religion, or gambling. You could also discover some unrealistic attachments to security or to power, resulting in the *tightwad* or *spendthrift* syndromes, respectively. This book will help you become aware of any psychological obstacles and deal with them.

Dealing with these psychological obstacles can be scary, but it is also a wonderful opportunity. Each time you eliminate one of these obstacles, you increase your choices. Preserving and cherishing your power of choice is foremost in our plan.

The power of choice will reveal itself financially and emotionally. Financially, you will see your assets increase, your liabilities decrease, and your spendable funds put into perspective by you. You will control your dollars, make your choices, and get what you want out of life. Emotionally, you will feel powerful, you will lose your anxiety, you will have a sense that you are nurturing yourself, and you will feel grounded in reality. And, when you work in a reality-based system in one area of your life, the effects will be so satisfying that we feel it will encourage you to ground yourself in other areas, thereby extending the sense of balance and power to the rest of your life.

So, we invite you to enjoy the simplicity of our financial plan and appreciate the new insights about yourself that following this plan may generate. The plan is set forth in a simple, step-by-step format. The psychological obstacles that may inhibit the progress of your plan are described throughout the book, and the case studies will illustrate both the financial and psychological sides of managing money.

Now, we'd like to answer one more question in this introduction: Why write this book for women? We certainly feel that men could benefit equally from our plan and from the psychological insights using this plan will uncover. We found that men labor within the same false systems as the ones we will describe, although it is our experience that they seem less aware of the emotional side of money and far less willing to confront the emotional obstacles that arise.

But we chose to write this book for women because we found that women very frequently labor under a myth that men are not subject to: *if you're a good girl, you'll be taken care of.* This was and is perhaps the most damaging and destructive myth of all those we have mentioned.

Being "good" very simply means *never having your own agenda*—it means taking care of others and not taking care of yourself. (If you're a good girl, someone else will do that for you.) Women are raised to believe that the system, whether it's administered by parents, husbands, families, bosses, or government, has their best interest at heart.

The reality is that women do very poorly under our political and economic systems. Women earn about 65 percent of what men earn, few women hold high positions in politics or business, and women live in poverty, along with their children, far more frequently than men do. Many women who have relied on marriage to fulfill their needs find that when they become divorced or widowed their husband's regard for them did not include taking care of them in his absence. Many female employees who have relied on their bosses to take care of them have been severely disappointed to see less qualified men promoted above them, or to see their request for a raise denied.

The only way to increase your chances of having a financially comfortable life is to establish your own agenda. Even if you've got the most loving parents, a caring and considerate partner, and a fabulous boss, it is critical that you have your own agenda and become your own advocate. We feel that gaining control over your finances is the first step.

Because of the political and economic obstacles that confront women, women simply have less money than men. And while we recognize that women do a remarkable job with the money they are able to earn, we also recognize the need for women to become more aware of the monetary inequities they face, of the myths that keep them from establishing and accomplishing their goals, and of the choices available to them. It is our personal goal that this book help women empower themselves financially and in other areas of their lives.

We hope that you will soon stop living from paycheck to paycheck, and begin your rise *From Paycheck to Power.*

Getting Started

Writing checks, making deposits, and paying bills are all financial activities. Discussing money, thinking about money, determining the uses of money, and, finally, planning the control of your money are all highly-charged, totally emotional activities. So the first step in getting started is this: Don't be fooled. Don't fool yourself into thinking that your emotions will play no role in your financial efforts. For most people, in most cases, emotions will play an enormous role.

You will need to get started in two ways: financially and psychologically. One is as important as the other, and both are inextricably linked. There is no magic in our plan. On the financial side, if you have incurred $10,000 of debt over the years, no plan will eliminate the fact that you owe $10,000. Only paying $10,000 will do that. Our plan will set you on the right track, though, and you will begin to pay off your debts in a reasonable, non-threatening way that will be equally agreeable to you and your creditors. On the emotional side, we urge you to be honest, even when you don't find the truth to be all that attractive. We implore you to honor yourself. Honor your desires, your strengths, your weaknesses, your capabilities and your deficiencies. Meet and honor yourself where you are today. Honor the person you are right now. Accept yourself. Don't waste even one second chastising yourself for not making more money or for not having less debt. Above all, do not allow yourself to fall into the "what if" trap. It is very easy to see the errors of the past when the future is the present. You are not in the business of abusing yourself. You are in the business of caring about you.

Preparing for the financial side of the plan is simple. The only tools you will need are: a checking account, a savings account, a pencil, a piece of paper, and a calculator. The math needed is limited to addition, subtraction, multiplication, division, fractions and percentages. If you have trouble with these computations, or do not have a pocket calculator, line up a friend to help you. If you have trouble organizing or sorting out your personal papers, you might think again about asking a trusted friend for help.

When you first begin the plan, you may experience a few initial setbacks. Don't be surprised and don't panic. The month after one of our clients started her plan, the air conditioning unit on her house went out ($130), she had to pay for a licensing test ($40), and she incurred a doctor's bill ($80) which was not covered by her medical insurance. She had no savings and no available credit.

If you suffer initial setbacks, tell yourself very firmly that these things will not happen every month. In fact, they may happen only once. After a moment of panic, our client spent some time figuring out how to fit these expenditures into her plan. She arranged with her repairman and doctor to pay the bills out over time; she spent her food and entertainment money on the licensing fee; she cut her living expenses drastically for a few weeks by foregoing restaurants in favor of eating what was in her freezer or on her shelves; and she entertained herself, without cost, by watching television, visiting friends, reading books, and taking walks. Our client found she could handle the setbacks she faced and not allow them to disrupt her plan. Again, the financial side of the plan is simple, and even though unexpected expenditures may arise, you simply need to fit them into your plan and proceed.

To prepare for the psychological side of money management, we'd like you to become an observer—an observer of yourself. The goal is to increase your awareness in many areas, and this will not be possible unless you make a commitment to observing your behavior and your feelings, and to identifying those behaviors and feelings that contribute to good money management and an overall sense of empowerment, in contrast to those that do not.

On the positive side, you will become aware of your good decisions that enhance your money management. You will probably become aware (most of our clients do) that your basic expenditures for rent or house payment, car, and food are reasonable. You may find that all of your expenditures are reasonable, and that a money crunch is due to timing problems, which the plan will straighten out. If so, congratulate yourself.

On the negative side, try to be aware of all your emotional reactions to decisions you make to reduce expenditures. If you have strong negative reactions to following your own rational decisions, or if you feel an irresistible impulse to spend money not allowed for in your plan, you are probably dealing with an addiction or a compulsion. Again, congratulate yourself on your self-awareness—and read Chapter 10, Compulsions and Addictions.

In fact, developing a plan may identify some compulsions or addictions. Part of the plan calls for looking at all of your expenditures for a month. One of our clients discovered, upon reviewing her checkbook for the first time in several months, that in the course of one thirty-day period she had written checks for more than $80 to her local liquor store. At first she was shocked that the checks totalled that amount. But then she began to examine her cancelled checks for other months, only to discover that the amount of money she spent on liquor purchases, and, in fact, the amount of liquor she was actually consuming, was a great deal more than she had ever realized. She took our advice and congratulated herself on the awareness and proceeded immediately to examine that aspect of her life.

Psychologically, most of you will find that you have been viewing money in an unrealistic and mythical way. The concept that spending money equals power is a prevalent misconception. The idea that controlling expenses is the same as deprivation is also a false equation that prohibits many people from even beginning any kind of money management. We found that, for women, perhaps the most commonly held myth was that almost anybody else's decision was better than their own. No one is in a better position to make decisions about you than you are. Only you know exactly what you need, what you fear, what brings you joy, what gives you hope, what makes your life your own. Relinquishing the power of decision-making (the power of choice) is the ultimate disregard of yourself. Always treat yourself with respect.

Whatever you find will be good. It will be something you will be pleased with or something you will find you wish to change, but in either case, you will be giving yourself the gift of awareness, and therefore, the gift of choice. You will learn to increase your assets and to decrease your liabilities; you will learn to respect and to nurture yourself. You will learn that money is neither good nor bad; it is neutral. You will find that there is no more reason to attach money to fear than to pride. And you will stop playing the role of victim. You will begin caring for yourself as well as someone who loved you greatly would care for you.

Finally, enjoy the sense of power and accomplishment you will have as you work your way through each and every step of the plan.

CHAPTER TWO

The Plan

The purpose of this chapter is to give you an overview of what's to come. Through this chapter and the ones following, we will take you, step-by-step, through the plan, as we would take a client through a counseling session. A glossary is provided at the end of the book for terms you may find unfamiliar.

So let's start at the beginning. It is difficult to reach your destination if you have no idea where you are now. Well, where are you? What is your present location financially and psychologically?

We feel that the best way to determine your present financial location is to examine the following areas:

- income
- fixed expenses
- controllable expenses
- savings
- retirement funds
- credit condition

The following six chapters will show you how to examine each of these areas in your current situation, and how to make the best decisions about each from now on.

Determining your present psychological location may not be quite as easy and straightforward because many of your psychological attributes often are not part of your conscious awareness. We hope to bring these attributes into your conscious awareness as a by-product of this plan.

At this time, you may want to list any psychological attributes of which you are already aware, such as

- a need to control
- a desire to be cared for
- a wish to be irresponsible
- "a fear of ..."
- "an addiction or compulsion to ..."

Depending on how your list turns out, you may find that one or more of these qualities will hinder the plan's success. This may not be the time for you to deal with such a problem, and if that's the case, then continue with your plan and perhaps you will find the courage to deal with these obstacles later. The chapter on compulsions and addictions may help you with this stage of the overall process.

While you are examining where you are financially and psychologically, we'd like you to examine one more myth. In our experience, this is probably the most frequently and consistently believed misconception:

- We *can* control our income.
- We *can't* control our expenses.
- We *can't* control the psychological factors.

The plan we set forth is based on the opposite of that myth. We ask you to assume that your income is fixed, but that you can control your expenses and change the psychological factors that hamper good financial management. We know you can—we've seen it happen!

Assume your income is fixed. The number of clients we counsel who feel they can control their income as a means of solving their financial problems is amazing. Nothing could be further from the truth. The reality is they can only control their income to the extent that they make a decision to change jobs, take a second job, quit a part-time job, resign, or negotiate. These choices are available to them. However, as long as they are employees, the ultimate control of their income is in the hands of their employer. This does not have to be a frightening fact; it is just a fact. Let yourself be aware of this.

However, while you need to assume that your income is fixed, be equally aware that you can have a lot of power over what you do for a living, especially if you have your finances under control. You may have the goal of increasing your income, yet be willing to take a temporary reduction in income while you go to school or start a business. Or you may wish to pursue a career that will reduce your income. You will find that, after you implement your plan and obtain control of your finances, you will have many more choices about your level of income. You will also have bigger financial reserves. These factors will give you more choices about what you will do for a living and greater confidence in determining what risks you can afford to take.

Many of our clients make changes in their work after implementing a financial plan. A psychologist and a lawyer each reduced their employment and increased their private practice.

Another woman left her employment permanently to become a writer and money-management counselor. Women frequently learn how their households can be managed on their partner's paycheck so they can stay home with their children. Always know what you want to do, and keep trying to do it. However, as long as you are an employee, look on your income as the least controllable of the three factors of money management.

You can control your expenses. Again, a surprising number of our clients believe their expenses cannot be controlled. Many people do not feel they have a choice to sell their house, or to buy a less expensive car, or to send their children to a moderately priced college. Frequently, clients will pay exorbitant rates for services they hardly use, yet feel powerless to eliminate the services. One of our clients listed a monthly payment of more than $60 to the cable TV service. She told us she resented paying the cable company that much. We asked her why she continued to keep the cable. She said her children had watched the movie channels but that, since she bought a VCR about three months earlier, they were renting movies and watching much less TV. Several months later, she finally had her cable service reduced to a monthly bill of less than $20, saving more than $40 per month thereafter. To her, and to some of you, that may not seem like a lot of money; but you have to assume (and it is the case) that many of her expenses reflected the same lack of thought. Add up very many of these "little" choices, and the disappearing dollars are enough to ruin anyone's finances.

Your power of choice is never more evident than in terms of expenses. You make the decision to incur the expense and you can make the decision to eliminate it. You can make the decision to sell a house not suited to you just as easily as you made the decision to buy it. You can select a car priced at $10,000 as readily as you select one priced at $30,000. All that stands between you and your decisions is your power of choice.

You *can* control the psychological factors. The psychological factors are generally believed to be the most difficult to change. Most people believe they cannot change their fears, desires, addictions, or compulsions. The truth is, however, that everyone has the capacity to grow and change, and many people do resolve their psychological dilemmas, and regain their power of choice.

All your addictions, compulsions and obsessions are the result of emotional and psychological traumas that you suffered when you were powerless to control your life. They are all mechanisms designed by your psyche to protect you from pain. The facts of the past cannot be obliterated. You cannot pretend you have not suffered these traumas. You cannot "not" know something, once you know it. You may no longer need the protection of your addictions, obsessions and compulsions, but your psyche doesn't know that, and it wants to protect you at all costs.

But whether you allow it to continue to protect you, to work under the illusion that you still need protection, is completely and utterly your decision. Only you allow your psyche to continue functioning in a mythical system. Only you give or withhold credence to those old fears. Coming to grips with the flaws in your present strategy is a tall order. And above all, we ask that you be kind and supportive of yourself, and that you gather a network of support people on whom you can rely. We also suggest that you seek professional counseling help if the task seems too great to handle alone.

To summarize, you have only limited control over your income, but you have quite a bit of control over your expenses, and even more control over your psychological issues. The reality in each case is this: you have the power of choice.

In conclusion, your goal in undertaking this plan will be twofold: Financially, you will strive to build your assets, reduce your expenses and manage each expense as cost-effectively as you possibly can. Psychologically, you will strive to eliminate old myths, replace them with realistic belief systems, and continue to grow into a person of balance, who has the power of choice.

CHAPTER THREE

Income

In this chapter, we define two basic types of income, baseline monthly income and acceleration income. *Baseline monthly income* is income you expect to receive reliably every month (for example, your paycheck). *Acceleration income* is money that does not arrive reliably every month, such as a tax refund or unexpected, overtime pay. We call it acceleration income because it helps you *accelerate* your plan. We will further define these types of income and show you how to maximize your income within the parameters of your current situation. First, we will have you identify the sources of your income. Second, we will ask you to examine the amount and when items of income are received. Third, we will take a look at your paycheck and show you how to maximize the amount of money you receive from that source. Finally, we will look at other income you might have.

Sources of Income

Identifying and examining all sources of income can reveal some surprising information. We had one client who had not balanced her checkbook in several months. We told her that one of her first tasks would be to balance her checking account against her most recent bank statement to determine precisely how much money she had available. She found that her checking account balance was actually $40 more than she thought it was.

Similarly, another client used his automobile in his job. He did some traveling each week and was reimbursed once a month at a set rate of twenty-six cents per mile. We asked him what he did with that check each month. He replied that he cashed it, but couldn't really say what he did with it. One thing was sure: it was not used to offset car expenses. It was a source of unmonitored income.

The most common sources of income are

- salary (paycheck)
- bonuses
- mileage reimbursements
- overtime pay
- alimony
- child support
- income earned from side-line business
- money earned from hobbies
- money earned from the sale of possessions
- insurance reimbursements
- monetary gifts
- tax refunds
- lump sum pension plan payments

- disability income
- welfare income (AFDC)
- supplemental security income (SSI)
- social security income
- retirement benefits
- windfalls

As you examine each item of income on our list, realize that each item which applies to you is your income, to use or misuse. Also realize that every dollar is the same as every other dollar. There are not some dollars that are worth less than others, which are appropriate to "blow." Most of our clients regarded their income tax refunds as "free money," to be spent without thought or control. But that money is worth exactly the same as any other money, and should be spent or saved with the same thought and consideration as regular paychecks.

How Much and When

Look at each item on our list carefully. Many of them may not apply to you, or you may have a source of income we have not listed. The important thing is to determine the minimum amount of money that comes to you in the course of one month, and when it arrives.

When do you receive money? Do you receive your paychecks once a month, once a week, twice a month, or every other week? Do your child-support payments arrive sporadically or like clockwork? Is the turnaround time on insurance reimbursements within reasonable limits, such as thirty days? Are you paid alimony, and, if so, does the check arrive dependably, at the same time each month? Does your company have you on a bonus plan that is attainable and, if you attain the goals, does it promptly pay you the correct amount? Do you receive monetary gifts from parents or loved ones on a regular basis? All of these questions have two parts to them: How much, and when?

Divide your income into baseline monthly income and acceleration income. Once you have made your list of all possible sources of income, look at each item of income on your original list from the perspective of whether it is money that arrives in the same amount every month, whether it fluctuates, or whether it is irregular, once-a-year or once-a-lifetime money. Then divide your list even further. Your income sources will fall into two categories: baseline monthly income and acceleration income.

Baseline monthly income is the income you expect to receive reliably each month. An example of this would be your paycheck. This is the money you will use to pay your fixed and most, or all, of your controllable expenses (see next two chapters).

Acceleration income is money that does not arrive reliably every month, such as money earned from the sale of possessions, an overtime check, or a tax refund. If you are paid every week, then four months a year you will receive a fifth check. If you are paid every other week, you will receive a third check two months out of the year. Because these extra checks are not received every month, they are acceleration income as well, that is, income that will literally help you accelerate the success of your plan.

Your new list may look something like this:

Baseline Income	Acceleration Income
Salary	Sale of possessions
Bonus	Tax refund
Alimony	Mileage reimbursement
Monetary gift	

Complete your list. Now, we'd like you to embellish your list just a bit more. Beside each item of income, place the date when this income arrives. For example, you may be paid your salary on the 1st and the 15th of each month. You receive a regular bonus check on the 30th of each month without fail. Your ex-husband is dependable, and those alimony checks are at your house on the 10th of every month. And there's wonderful Aunt Agatha who has been sending you $100 on the first of every month for the last thirty years just because you're her favorite niece. In addition, on the acceleration side, the family annual garage sale is a neighborhood event held on the 1st of June.

The IRS usually pays you back some money around April, so long as you file your return without delay; and when you travel for your company, those mileage checks are cut on the 20th of each month, so long as you've submitted your report by the 10th. So now let's look at your list.

Baseline Income	Acceleration Income
Salary, 1st and 15th	Sale of possessions, June
Bonus, 30th	Tax refund, April
Alimony, 10th	Mileage reimbrsmnt., 20th
Monetary gift, 5th	

Timing is a critical factor. Many people have big bucks for one week and starve the other three. Timing is equally important when discussing "money coming in" as when discussing "money going out." Don't underestimate the significance of when you perform financial transactions. In many cases you will find that when is more important than how much. You will see why when you read Chapters 4 and 5 on Fixed Expenses and Controllable Expenses.

Now we will briefly examine each potential source of income. First, we will look at your paycheck, and show you ways to increase the amount of your take-home pay; then we will look at other sources of income.

Your Paycheck

All of you who are employed will have a minimum base salary. Don't consider your monthly income to be the gross amount before deduction; consider your income to be the net amount after all deductions—otherwise known as your take-home pay. This is the dollar amount that is actually in your check.

And speaking of your check, let's look at it carefully. Let's examine the difference between the gross amount and the net, take-home amount. Everyone will usually have two deductions (federal income tax and FICA) and many of you will also have a state income tax withholding. Some of you may have a city or local withholding tax.

Tax Withholding

If you receive a large tax refund each year, say $1,000 or more, you are having more tax withheld from your paycheck than you really need to. You can choose to reduce your withholding (and increase the size of your paycheck), but it may be a little tricky getting the change through your payroll office. This is not because it's illegal. It is because systems, especially companies, don't like changes. What you need to do is this: obtain a Form W-4, either from your payroll office or from an IRS office. Fill out the form entirely, especially the worksheet that asks about your income and deductions. (If necessary, get help—possibly from your regular tax preparer—in filling out this form). When you have finished filling it out, you will see that you are entitled to claim more "exemptions" on your W-4 than you have been claiming. Give the W-4 form (not the worksheet) to your paymaster, and the company will be required to reduce your withholding.

Of course, if you do this, you will not receive a large refund at tax time. So, remember—make a choice!

Many people see their big tax refund each year as a savings plan, and they literally put the check into their savings account as soon as it arrives. If this method gives you more peace of mind than seeing the extra money in your check each week, stick with it. Never feel ambivalent about money saved—as long as it's done in a balanced way, it is always good for you.

While we are talking about refunds, we want to warn you against cheating on your taxes. If you claim deductions you are not entitled to, you can go to jail and be required to pay substantial penalties. It's not worth it. Keep your finances in order, and the temptation to cheat on your taxes will diminish.

Deductions Other Than Tax Withholding

Basically, after withholding taxes, the remaining deductions in your check, if you have them, are ones you control.

For example, we examined one client's check and found he had a deduction of $18 per paycheck for which we couldn't account. He returned to work and asked the paymaster, only to find that he had signed up for a charitable contribution a year and a half earlier that was still being taken out of each check. Another client, who was employed by a large resort, had numerous deductions because she could charge at the restaurants, sports shop and gift shop. With such easy access to acquiring goods and services in a system where no money actually changed hands, this client was being plagued by deductions. These purchases, which were so easily made, were seriously decreasing her take-home pay. Another client worked for a company that had an in-house credit union service. Because of the way she handled her money, she frequently was without funds, and developed the habit of borrowing small amounts from the credit union to tide her over. The payback became increasingly more difficult as her paycheck began to shrink because of credit union deductions.

Union Dues

Union dues are another source of deduction that you may or may not be able to alter. If you work in a "closed shop," then you must be a member of the union, and you must pay the union dues. If it is not a closed shop, then you have a choice. You may find that being a member of the union will have advantages for you, or you may find that it isn't your cup of tea; in either case, don't overlook the fact that you have a choice.

Charitable Deductions

One of the deductions we found frequently had psychological overtones was the charitable contribution. For the record, let us say that we support cash contributions to the charities of your choice, as well as contributions of time and effort. We never ask clients to set aside those causes about which they feel strongly. However, it has been our experience that, with a few exceptions, most charitable contributions that are payroll deducted are based more on peer pressure or the seeking-approval expense than on a heartfelt desire to contribute to a particular cause or organization. Don't fall into this trap! We had a client who was not able to meet his household obligations each month (paying utility bills, for example) and yet was having more than $150 per month deducted for various charitable causes. We asked him if he felt strongly about continuing these contributions, or if he would feel comfortable putting a freeze on them until he got his own finances in order. He confessed that he didn't even know which charities were included in his deductions or where his money was going. He had signed up for them because he felt a person in his position at the company had to maintain a certain status, and contributing was highly regarded at this firm. If your contributions are based on guilt, the fear of disapproval, or the desire to maintain an image and not on a desire to fund an organization you believe in, then step back and take a realistic look at your decisions. If your finances are in chaos, yet you use money to alleviate the pressure you feel others are putting on you, ask yourself if these decisions are in your own best interest. It's definitely time to think about you rather than what others may think of you.

Until you get your personal finances in order, we recommend that you suspend all cash charitable contributions. Resuming these contributions is a reward you can give yourself when you are comfortably meeting your personal needs and obligations. Remember, if you follow your plan, you will find yourself in a very comfortable financial position, and will be able to do more for your favorite charities than if you remain in a tenuous financial position.

Health Insurance Deductions

Another deduction you might take a look at is a deduction for health insurance coverage. If you are married, and your husband has medical insurance coverage, both of you do not have to pay for a family plan. Each member of the family needs to be covered by only one policy. Compare the benefits and expenses, and select the best policy for your family. However, be sure you and your husband are both covered by disability as well as by medical insurance, if it is available. Although it is rare for an insurance company to cover an unmarried partner, the same guidelines would apply.

Retirement Plan Deductions

We believe a substantial amount of your income should be devoted to a retirement plan. But retirement planning should be kept in balance. As you develop your plan, you may need to reduce or suspend your retirement deductions temporarily, resuming them at a specific date in the near future.

Bonuses

If you are on a bonus plan that pays monthly, include an estimated minimum amount in your monthly income. However, unless you are absolutely sure you will receive this bonus every month, don't count it. If it pays less often than monthly, treat it as acceleration income and do not include it in your baseline monthly amount. If you are a waiter and most of your income is from tips, include the minimum amount that you typically receive per month.

Other Income

After you have carefully examined your paycheck, you should then consider all other sources of income, which may come your way.

Mileage

If travelling is part of your job, then mileage will be part of your income. Again, count this income as baseline income only if you receive a check each month. If travelling is an "every-now-and-then" part of your job, count these checks as acceleration income.

Overtime

Many jobs will advertise, as their selling point, overtime wages. Overtime is normally at least "time and one-half" per hour, so your wages can be dramatically increased by working over-time. What frequently happens, however, is that the company is reluctant to request overtime work because of the cost; so your salary becomes only the base salary at which you were hired. Don't fool yourself. If your base salary is $250 a week and you are hardly ever requested to work overtime, be realistic and place those occasional overtime wages in the acceleration category.

Alimony

Alimony is money paid by one spouse to the other as part of the divorce agreement. If you are required to pay alimony, this amount becomes one of your fixed expenses; if you are the recipient of alimony, and it arrives without fail on the specified day, then it becomes part of your baseline monthly income. If you are entitled to alimony by virtue of the divorce agreement, but your ex-spouse fails to send you the check, then that money, when and if it arrives, becomes part of your acceleration income.

Child Support

If you legally should receive child support but your ex-husband never quite gets around to writing the check, don't count it. If it doesn't come to you and you can't depend on receiving it, you do not have the use of it—therefore, it belongs in the acceleration category if and when it ever shows up. With the system of child support being what it is, and the number of fathers who do not support their own children on the rise, don't pretend your income is something it isn't. You may be entitled to that extra $500 per month, but if you never see it, it isn't income.

Treat child support the same as any other income. There is no need to use child-support checks solely for direct expenses of the child. The court system recognizes that a large portion of child support needs to go to the overall expense of the household where the child resides.

Side-Line Business

If you have a side-line business in addition to your regular job, we wish to point out two things: (1) Consider the money you make from this business to be baseline income only if you generate it on a regular basis—otherwise, consider it to be acceleration income; and (2) Obtain the services of an accountant to aid you in record keeping of the tax liability you may be incurring. The money you make from your side-line business is considered income for tax purposes just like the money you get from your regular job. Don't shoot yourself in the foot by generating a nice side-line income only to lose it by having to pay delinquent taxes and penalties.

Hobbies

Technically, the money generated by hobbies also is considered income for tax purposes, so again, consult a professional regarding record keeping. Also, remember to include this income in your baseline income list only if your hobby produces income each month.

Sale of Possessions

Everyone has had the occasional garage sale. Normally, this is exclusively acceleration income, even if you hold the event once a year faithfully. If you've never held a garage sale, try it. Cleaning out the possessions that pile up over the years can give you a feeling of accomplishment and freedom, and make you feel very light. We suggest this activity even if you choose to donate all the discarded possessions to a charitable organization (and take the tax deduction). It also helps to take an inventory every once in a while.

Insurance Reimbursement

If an insurance reimbursement is for damage to your home or car, use it only to repair or replace damaged or stolen items. If you do not use it for that purpose, count it as acceleration income.

If the insurance reimbursement is for medical expenses, and you have already paid the doctor, it is income, to be paid back to you or to be placed in the acceleration category. If you have not yet paid the doctor, it is not your money; it is the doctor's. Do not even deposit it in your account. Turn it over and write on the back, "Pay to the order of Dr. _____" and sign your name. Then put it in an envelope and mail it to the doctor. (Many people incur totally unnecessary medical debts because they cash their medical insurance checks and spend the money on something other than the medical bills.)

Monetary Gifts

Very few people we know receive monetary gifts, but some do. Those who receive these gifts from loved ones normally receive them occasionally, out of the blue. In this case, when they are received unexpectedly, they are to be considered acceleration income. Sometimes, the grandmother who just happens to have the same first name as you have will send you a cash gift every Christmas or on your birthday or on some other special date. This is acceleration income. This doesn't mean you can't take the money and spend it on yourself. It simply means that you should see it as a choice that you make. You can spend it, you can save it, or you can use it to further your plan.

Tax Refunds

Tax refunds are possibly the best regular source of acceleration income. We have had clients completely change their financial picture because they made excellent use of a tax refund, which they ordinarily would have blown without a second thought. Give great consideration to the way you use such income, especially if it's a large amount that could mean the difference between indebtedness and solvency.

Lump Sum Pension Plan Payments

If you leave your job and are entitled to money from your pension plan, or have funded a 401K savings plan, you will receive a check that may be quite large. Many people cash these checks and spend them. Then, when tax time rolls around, they find they have a large tax liability for the pension-plan or savings-plan money that they spent as income. The best thing to do is to continue to treat this as retirement money, and invest it in an IRA (Individual Retirement Account) within sixty days of receipt. This is called a "roll-over" and will eliminate any taxes on this money, as well as provide a nice retirement fund. Any bank will be happy to set up an IRA for you.

Disability Income, AFDC, SSI, Social Security

If you receive private disability insurance payments, or income from governmental sources, such as AFDC (Aid to Families with Dependent Children), SSI (Supplemental Security Income), or Social Security, these checks become your primary baseline income, and, in some cases, they are all you are receiving. Don't feel like you can't establish a plan because you're not employed or because you receive this assistance. It doesn't matter where your money comes from—what matters is what you do with it. You can utilize your AFDC check as efficiently as a paycheck. If you have trouble receiving your checks, do not hesitate to seek legal assistance through the local legal aid service. You depend on this money to live, just as you would depend on your paycheck if you were employed. If your check should arrive on the 5th of each month but you don't receive it until the 12th, or if it is the wrong amount, then go through the necessary channels to correct the errors. If you can't get anyone to help you, look up your state's legal assistance organization in your phone book and make an appointment. The lawyers there will be able to help you. It is the law.

We recognize that obtaining and maximizing your benefits can be practically a full-time job. Since it is your primary source of income, be very serious about doing everything you can to maximize your income and use it wisely.

Retirement

If you are receiving retirement income, that means two things: (1) You have done a very good job over the years of saving, or you wouldn't be retired; and (2) The retirement income is your baseline monthly income and you should develop your plan with that in mind.

Windfalls

Windfalls are truly occasional and unexpected. You hit the lottery; your great uncle, whom you've never met, dies and leaves you all his money; you write a book for fun in your spare time and it becomes a bestseller, much to your surprise—these are examples of windfalls. Again, the important thing to remember is that you have choices. You can spend the money in record-breaking time, you can save it, you can save part of it, or you can use it to accelerate your plan. The choice is yours, but some choices are clearly in your best interest and some are not. We'd like you to remember that a big point of this book is teaching you how to recognize the difference, and to act accordingly.

All of These Suggestions Add Up to One Goal

Maximize your income! This doesn't mean you should rush out and find a new job that pays more. This means that you should scrutinize your income from a new position—a position of being as good to yourself as you can. Ask yourself if the decisions you're living with are the best for you. Are all those deductions in your paycheck ones you feel good about? Are you doing everything you can to ensure that your bonus check arrives on time, or that your alimony or child-support checks are in your mailbox when they're supposed to be, or that the insurance reimbursement is not being held up because you didn't follow through on something? See these tasks in a new light. Each time you make the decision to take more control and to maximize your income, you are being good to yourself. You are treating yourself with respect. You are honoring your own wishes.

Each time you ignore your power of choice, each time you allow an opportunity for choice to slip by, you disregard yourself.

You send a clear message to your subconscious that you are not worth recognizing, not worth taking the time for. You would never treat your own child that way, and you should never treat yourself that way.

So let's look at that income one more time. And don't let the system discourage you. The system—of companies, courts, or charities—is set up to discourage change. The red tape can suppress individual desires rather than aid in their fulfillment. You must be your own champion and cut through the red tape. Don't miss even one opportunity.

CHAPTER FOUR

Fixed Expenses

Now that you've determined your total income and divided it into baseline monthly income and acceleration income, the next step is to make a realistic examination of your *fixed expenses*. This is not at all hard to do. Our system for managing fixed expenses is based on three factors: reducing, levelizing, and timing. We discuss reducing expenses throughout the book; this chapter focuses on levelizing and timing. The first step is to identify your fixed expenses. Then, we will show you techniques to reduce and levelize your fixed expenses. Third, we will show you how to arrange the timing of your fixed expenses to pay them when you get paid. Finally, there is a special section for those of you who are paid monthly, weekly or biweekly.

Identify Your Fixed Expenses

Fixed expenses are those over which you have very little control; they are fixed by someone or something else. For example, you cannot control the amount of your rent or mortgage payment except by moving. Once you've made your choice of a residence, the rent is set by the property owner, or the amount of the mortgage is set at the time you buy the house.

The most common fixed expenses are

- rent/mortgage
- utilities (electricity, gas, water, garbage, sewer)
- phone (local service, long distance service)
- cable TV (basic cable service, premium channels)
- insurance (house/apartment, car, medical, life)
- taxes (real estate, personal property)
- loans (car, consumer, student, specific item loans)
- newspaper delivery

This list will, no doubt, look very familiar to you. Everyone pays rent, utility bills, car insurance, and several other items listed. But we'd like to draw your attention to two points in particular:

1. We do not include credit or charge cards as fixed expenses. They are controllable by you and are not a set amount, with a set pay-off date. Treat them as *controllable expenses,* which are dealt with in the next chapter. (When we say "credit card" we mean Visa, MasterCard, American Express, and so forth. When we use the term "charge card" we are referring to such things as a gasoline charge card or a department store charge card.)

2. Your fixed expenses should total no more than a maximum of two-thirds or roughly 65 percent of your baseline monthly income. Ideally, direct your efforts toward keeping those fixed expenses as far below the 65 percent mark as possible. The lower the percentage of fixed expenses, the more comfortable you will be financially. For example, if your baseline income was $1,500

per month, you'd want to keep your fixed expenses below $975 per month (65 percent of $1,500 equals $975).

Before you begin to panic and worry about your fixed expenses and whether they are too high, take some time to gather the information you will need in order to make a sound decision.

Go through your check registers and make a list of all bills you receive every month without fail and all bills you have to pay every month just to run your household. Do *not* include credit or charge-card debt or food at this time. For each bill, write down the company and the amount. You will probably have to guess at the average bills for electricity and gas because they are different every month, but give it your best estimate.

Your list might look something like this:

    Rent $425
    Electric . . . . . .   60 average
    Gas . . . . 40 average
    Water . . . .   18 average
    Phone . . . .   25 basic service
                         10 long distance
    Loan—car . . . 175

Now, make another list. This will be a shorter list. Put down any bills you have to pay that are not sent to you monthly. For example, a six-month insurance premium bill, a quarterly tuition bill, or a quarterly tax payment.

Your second list could look like this:

    Insurance . . . . $540 every 6 months

Now we want to do all that we can to make as many factors constant as possible. Your baseline monthly income as we defined it in Chapter 3 is constant. And if our bills were constant, the process would be very, very simple. For example, if your paycheck were $1,000 a month, and your monthly fixed expenses were always $650, you would be safe in assuming that you would have $350 to yourself after each bill was paid. Unfortunately, that isn't how it works. Our incomes are usually painfully constant; it's our expenses we can't seem to make stand still. Or can we?

We'd like to show you that there are a few easy steps you can take that will make your expenses constant—no surprises. To the extent that it is possible, we want you to control your fixed expenses.

Reducing and Levelizing Your Fixed Expenses

Now that you have identified your fixed expenses, your next job is to reduce and levelize those expenses so they will be exactly the same amount every month.

Mortgage

While mortgages are fixed expenses for purposes of this book, sometimes the monthly payment can be reduced by refinancing the mortgage. Monthly mortgage payments are reduced in two ways: by lowering the interest rate, (a rule of thumb is two percentage points lower than the present interest rate on your mortgage); or by spreading your payments over a longer period of time.

Be aware, however, that you will not only want to shop around to get the lowest mortgage interest rate you can, but you will also incur closing costs when you refinance a mortgage. The money you would expend in closing costs needs to be balanced against the money you would save in monthly payments. If you think refinancing may be a good choice for you, talk to several mortgage loan officers to get the facts.

Utility Bills

Let's look at the utility companies. Contact these utilities and ask to be put on "levelized" billing. There is no charge for this, and, instead of getting a big surprise each month when you open these bills and find out if you can afford them, you will have an idea of how much they will be before you even get the bill. The utility companies certainly don't mind implementing this arrangement. It actually helps balance out their own cash flow. Each of your bills will still have the actual charges on it so there is no problem in determining the amount you are being charged, in case you think there's an error. Most companies will review the amounts of your bills for a six- or twelve-month period, average them out, and send you a bill that will show your actual amount for the month and the levelized amount that you should pay. If your overall usage for the six- or twelve-month period is less than average, your levelized amount will go down; if it is more than anticipated, your levelized amount will increase. The important thing, however, is that you will have eliminated, with only one phone call, those extraordinarily high heating or air conditioning bills that reflect a change in season but not a change in income.

Telephone (local service)
The next thing to do is to examine carefully the phone bill. Are you paying for services you are not using? Do you have more than one line coming into your house when you really only need one? Do you pay extra for call forwarding, or an unlisted number, or call waiting, or any other service the phone company offers that you may have needed, or thought you needed, at one time but don't use? You might be paying regular rate when measured service would be more economical (this is especially true if there are no children in the house, if you're not much of a phone user, or if you travel a lot and rarely use your home phone). The difference between regular rate and measured service can be the difference between a $30 phone bill and a $20 phone bill. Call the phone company to go over your bill and allow one of its representatives to explain exactly which services you receive and the cost of each one. Then make a good decision based on what you really want your phone to do.

Telephone (long-distance service)

Next, let's look at long-distance service. Since you now have the option of choosing which long-distance company handles your service, it would be foolish to give up the choice. Call AT&T, MCI, and Sprint (to name just a few) or any other long-distance company advertising in your area and ask about rates. It is especially important to examine your long-distance phone service if you live away from family and friends and your long-distance phone bills are real whoppers every month. Shop around and make sure you get what you want. It's one thing to pay for services you need and use; it's entirely another to pay for services you don't need and don't use.

Cable TV

We listed cable TV as a monthly fixed expense because so many households have it these days. Cable TV and VCRs seem to have become necessities for some families. So, let's look at cable. Personally, we love cable TV. But many of our clients pay for services they aren't using. Why pay for premium channels when you don't watch them because you have a VCR and can rent the same movies? Cutting out your premium channels will probably save you at least $10 per channel, per month—enough to rent several movies from the local video store. Take a good look at cable. Don't give up something you love—just don't pay for something you don't use.

Insurance

What is the purpose of insurance? Insurance is a financial line of defense against both foreseen and unforeseen events. There are many types of insurance, each serving a specific purpose and each guarding against a specific event. For example, we all buy car insurance to guard against loss resulting from a car accident. Other types of insurance are life, disability, liability (in case you get sued for injuring someone), property (on your home and personal possessions), and health.

Select a company and an agent you trust. The best way to select the right types and amounts of insurance is to choose a good agent and tell him or her what you want to accomplish. And while our aim in every case is to lower our fixed expenses, the intelligent choices are not always the ones with the lowest price tags. Nowhere is this more evident than with insurance. Fortunately, insurance is one of the few fixed expenses where you can easily choose whom to deal with. You should have an agent and a company you trust. The company will insure your home or apartment and your car, may perhaps insure you through medical coverage, and may insure your retirement and care for your loved ones through life insurance. Be extremely careful that the company you've selected is reputable and has a longstanding policy of conservative money management and primary care for its policy holders.

The most common method our clients used to select insurance companies was the "low ball" method. Most of our clients called three or four insurance companies and signed up with the one that offered the cheapest premiums. This is definitely not the best selection method. You need good service as well as a reasonable price.

The second most commonly used method was the "I knew a guy who knew a guy" method. The client knew someone who knew someone who was selling insurance, and so the client signed up, rather than exercising the right to choose a company based on factual data.

For good factual data, visit the reference room of your local library and review the *Consumer Reports*. This magazine examines insurance companies and rates them based on customer satisfaction. Ask the reference librarian for help in locating this publication if you're not familiar with the library.

Your agent will be your contact with the company you select. Don't underestimate the importance of choosing a good agent. Be completely certain your agent is a person whom you trust and with whom you enjoy transacting business. If you do not like the first agent you call, then change agents. This is neither a crime nor a difficult procedure. You're entitled to use any agent you want, and, if you don't like the one you've got, then keep searching.

Pay attention to your feelings. If you are presently dealing with an agent that treats you like you're stupid or who acts as though they don't appreciate your business, or if you're with a company that doesn't respond to claims promptly or handle your questions with courtesy and kindness, then we urge you to stop allowing yourself to be abused by them. If you get the feeling that you're disturbing your agent when you call, don't let the fact that the insurance rate might be $5 less than some other company influence you. Believe us, you will prefer paying $5 more to another company if you enjoy doing business with its personnel.

Many times an agent will seem very cooperative when selling you insurance and far less cooperative when you're making a claim. If that's the case, get rid of that agent immediately. Inefficiency is another big reason to change agents; if the nicest agent is inefficient or uncooperative when it comes to handling your claims or questions, go immediately to the yellow pages and find yourself someone who is competent. There are hundreds of agents representing every company, and some are willing to work very hard to get and keep your business. Why make the decision to give your business away to someone who isn't willing to do that?

If you feel you are in an equal relationship (which means that the company and agent you're dealing with are as grateful for the opportunity to do business with you as you are with them), you will feel powerful and respected.

Once you've settled on an insurance company and agent and have arranged to insure your home, apartment, car, medical, and/or life, we can look at the numbers.

Insurance can easily be levelized. Most insurance companies will be happy to put you on a monthly payment plan and send you a bill due on the same day each month. If you are presently paying your insurance premiums on an annual, semi-annual, or quarterly plan, call your agent and request that you be billed on the monthly plan. This will provide you with a set fee due each month to cover all your insurance needs, and will eliminate the panic you feel when all the premiums totalling several hundred dollars are due at once. There is usually a small service charge for monthly billing, but it's worth paying for the benefits you'll receive.

Most companies now have direct withdrawal of premiums. In this case you would authorize your insurance company to withdraw a set amount from your checking account each month, which would cover the cost of the total monthly premiums. This is done on the same day each month, a day that you select. So, select it with care. If you are always paid on the 15th of the month, but don't ever get to the bank until the 17th to deposit your check, don't let the insurance company withdraw from your account on the 16th. Think ahead and think in your own best interest. Also, most insurance companies will forego the small service charge for monthly billing if you go on direct withdrawal.

Select the right insurance for you. It is impossible for any book to declare flatly that one kind of insurance is superior to another. Many times you will hear people say, "Always buy term insurance," or "Never buy term insurance," or "Only buy this type of whole life insurance," or "Never buy this type." The truth is that each individual's situation is different. Some people are married, some are single, some live with a partner, some have children, some do not. The possibilities for human connections or the lack of them are numerous. So, you must realize that no one kind of product (whether it's insurance or cable or phone etc.) works for everyone. The key is to determine what you want your insurance to do before you go shopping. Change your attitude about purchasing. Don't "be sold" something like insurance; go out and "buy" the insurance you want, which fits your needs and requirements and does what you want it to do. Money you spend on accomplishing what you want is never wasted money. So, if you've learned all you can about a particular type of insurance and you're satisfied that it will do the things you want it to do (for instance, provide you with a retirement benefit or death benefit, or send your kids to college), be happy with your decision, and don't be undermined by what you may construe to be someone else's negative comments. He or she may be telling the truth about his own needs rather than being critical of your decisions.

Taxes

Most working women feel taxed to death. And there's a reason for that. It's true. You pay income tax to federal, state, and local governments, real estate tax on your house, personal property tax on your furniture, car and possessions, sales tax on all the items you buy; and let's not forget the ever-present social security tax. (Whether social security benefits will be available when it's time for you to receive them is another issue, and one that makes Chapter 7 on retirement all the more essential.)

With all the money you'll be legally required to hand over in taxes, the very least you can do is organize the payment of your taxes so that it causes you the least amount of stress.

Income Taxes. Conveniently, most employers withhold federal, state and local income tax through your paycheck. But you do have some choice here, as we mentioned in Chapter 3. Your choice centers around the number of exemptions you claim on your W-4 form. In deciding how much to have withheld, consider your peace of mind. If you feel more secure by having the maximum amount deducted from your paycheck and receiving a sizeable refund at tax time, then arrange or continue to do that. If you would have more peace of mind by having the minimum withheld and seeing the extra money in your check each payday, then arrange or continue to do that. All we ask of our clients is that they make this choice with awareness. If you have always had the minimum amount withheld and have tried to save a certain amount from your check for your own savings account, but have been unable to do this, then recognize this trend. You may have the best intentions, but if the facts show that you're not doing what you intend to do with the money, then your present plan isn't working and it's time to change it. Conversely, if you have the maximum withheld in the hopes of receiving a large refund to put in the bank toward your savings efforts, but for the last three years you've blown the check as soon as it arrived on items you can't even recall now, then, again, look honestly at what you're doing. Decide on your withholding tax based on a conscious awareness of your intentions, your desires, and your actions.

Real Estate Taxes and Personal Property Taxes. Real estate taxes are usually paid to your mortgage holder along with your mortgage payment. Your mortgage holder saves up these payments in an "escrow" account and pays the tax when it's due. If, however, you have paid off your mortgage, these taxes will probably be payable in one annual payment or four quarterly payments. If you have a choice, it probably will be easier for you to plan on quarterly payments than to try to save money all year for a once-a-year disbursement.

Similarly, personal property tax (if your state assesses it) usually cannot be paid on a monthly basis, and is paid either once a year, or through a specific number of installment payments per year. Levelizing the payments on these taxes is a little more difficult. We suggest two methods to our clients. Some actually calculate the monthly payment, write the check, and keep it in an envelope marked PERSONAL PROPERTY TAX until it's time to mail in the payment. There is no confusion, and when the tax is actually due, they simply mail the checks they have held in the envelope for that purpose. Others find it is best to treat personal property tax or real property tax as an extraordinary item and pay for it out of their "working savings." (See Chapter 6 on savings.)

If the personal property tax amount is small, many clients prefer to pay it in the installments arranged by the tax collector and absorb the cost into their controllable expenses. This will be explained further in the next chapter.

Other Taxes. Sales tax is a "pay-as-you-go" tax, and social security is withheld by your employer through your check. There are really no choices to be made in these areas.

In summation, taxes are obligations that cannot be avoided; but, if you find that you have some choice as to how and when taxes are paid, examine the options available to you and choose with your own best interest in mind.

Loans

We have an entire chapter on credit (Chapter 8), but we need to look at how credit decisions affect your fixed expenses. Borrowing money is a curious activity—few people ever realize, on an emotional level, that they actually have to pay it back. Oh, they sign the note and cash the check and readily admit that they now owe $15,000 for a car, $20,000 in student loans, or $10,000 for new furniture; but most of them never fully understand what that means until they begin to write the repayment checks each month.

There is no reason not to take out a loan for something you need. We urge you only to borrow money with an awareness of the effects that that loan will have on your financial well-being.

Most loans fall into the following categories:

- car loans
- consumer loans
- student loans
- specific item loans

Car Loans. There is nothing wrong with taking out a car loan. The problems arise when you take out a loan to buy a car that you can't afford; and by this we mean, one that places an undue burden on you to repay. In other words, buying that Ford may fit into your income without much stress, but buying the BMW can make you feel trapped—trapped into working to pay your car payment no matter what.

Consumer Loans. Consumer loans are usually made with banks or credit unions and are obtained for a variety of needs. Sometimes people wish to consolidate their bills or take a vacation or put in a new lawn… the list goes on and on.

Student Loans. Student loans seem to have the capability of depressing an entire generation well into their forties. Nearly every client we saw had a student loan of a "bazillion" dollars hanging over her head. These loans apparently have a half-life of one thousand years. They never go away. If your student loan payments are killing you, see Chapter 8, Credit, for some techniques to deal with overwhelming debt.

If you're considering taking out a student loan, remember that it takes a long time to repay $20,000 when your annual salary is $25,000. Many people sign up for student loans totalling that amount or more, as they obtain a degree that qualifies them for a job with a maximum starting salary of barely more than what they borrowed. Be conscious of the position you may be putting yourself in. Be aware of the financial stress you may be sentencing yourself to by the indebtedness you assume.

Specific Item Loans. We listed a category that we called "specific item" loans to designate the loans extended to customers for the purchase of items such as furniture, computers, or appliances for which the store arranges the financing.

These four types of loans all have several things in common. First, they all have a fixed monthly payment. You sign a note or an application for credit and the lender (such as a bank, credit union, store, or finance company) will tell you exactly how much to pay each month by sending you a bill or a coupon book. Second, in time, these loans do get paid off. This is the nicest feature about them.

Another important point about these loans is the interest rate. Become aware of interest rates! (Read Chapter 8, which goes into various types of loans and discusses interest in much greater detail.) Chapter 8 will show you how to manage your loans so they are less burdensome.

Newspaper Delivery

Newspaper delivery is usually a fairly small sum, but paying it once a year, as some newspaper companies prefer you to do, can mean, in one month out of twelve, coming up with $50 to $150 that you hadn't counted on. We advise that you pay the newspaper carrier once a month with a check. Many companies will run a special by offering you a discounted rate for payment for a full year. If that's the case, take them up on their offer, but beware. When the year is over and they call you to renew, the price usually increases to the regular rate, and at that point you'd be better off paying the carrier once a month again.

Savings

Please notice that we have devoted an entire chapter to savings (Chapter 6). We mention it here because we want you to become accustomed to treating savings as you would a fixed expense. If that sounds confusing, we'll try to clear it up.

The only difference between savings and other bills you pay is that savings is a bill you pay *to yourself.* An essential part of this plan is treating yourself with respect. Paying yourself through a savings account, which you will fund on a regular basis, is being very respectful and caring of *you.* We consider payment to *yourself* one of the most important components of our plan. We feel that the idea of funding savings accounts is so important that we want you to do it regularly, just like you pay your bills. It should never be overlooked; payments to the savings accounts should not be allowed to slip. You care about yourself and about your financial well-being, and funding savings accounts is one major way you send the message to yourself that you are completely worthy of that kind of care and attention.

Once you work out your plan, you will arrive at a specific amount per month to be paid to your savings account, and you will write that check just as you write your other checks to pay your bills. Even if your savings amount is only $5 per month when you first begin your plan, don't be discouraged. One of our clients had no savings when she came to us, but, upon working out her plan, she determined that she could afford to put $10 per month into a new account, which she opened. Within ten months, this client had increased her monthly savings amount from $10 to $100, had accumulated more than $1,000 in savings, and had started to fund an IRA at $25 per month as her first step in retirement planning. You can imagine how powerful she feels when she looks at what she has accomplished in less than a year.

Timing—How to Pay Your Bills When You Get Paid

One crucial element of your plan will be to *pay your bills when you get paid.* The following four-step method will show you how to do this.

1. List the Due Dates of Your Bills.

At this point you should have all your fixed expenses listed on a piece of paper in front of you. (Credit and charge card bills and food and gasoline should not be included in this list.)

Your list might look something like this:

Rent $425
Electric ......   60 average
Gas ....   40 average
Water ....   18 average
Phone ....   25 average basic local service
                10 average long distance service
Cable ....   20 basic service
Insurance ....   20 renter's insurance
                50 auto
                 0 medical (covered by employer)
                20 life insurance
Loans .... 175 car loans
               100 student loans
Newspaper ...   5 weekend subscription only
Savings ......   — (not yet determined)

Now, add up all these bills and get a total monthly amount to be paid for these fixed expenses. Also, write in the due dates of each bill. Remember, due dates represent the dates on which the money is due to arrive at the company, not the day you are to mail it. So, if your electric bill has a due date of the 22nd of each month, the money should be in the hands of the electric company by the 22nd, not leave your hands at that time.

Your new list might look like this:

Rent	$425	1st
Electric	60	22nd
Gas	40	10th
Water	18	28th
Phone	35	16th
Cable	20	18th
Insurance	90	25th
Loans	275	9th (car) 17th (student)
Newspaper . . .	5	30th
	$968	

2. Arrange to Pay Your Bills When You Get Paid.

As we mentioned earlier, timing is a critical element of the plan. And timing is a thing that you can control to your advantage. Now that you have your fixed expenses listed and due dates in place, let's look at your baseline monthly income, and *when* it arrives. Suppose you receive your paychecks on the 1st and on the 15th. If you're currently paying bills whenever they arrive, or holding them all until the last minute and then paying everything in one day, or whatever your present method is, change it to match when your income arrives. If you are paid once a month, pay bills once a month. If you are paid twice a month, pay bills on those days, and if you are paid once a week, pay bills once a week. *Pay your bills when you get paid.*

For purposes of this example, let's say your baseline monthly income (take-home pay) is $1,600, paid to you on the 1st and on the 15th, $800 each check.

Because you are paid twice a month, you will pay your bills twice a month, so let's now divide your total fixed expenses by two. ($968 divided by 2 = $484.) Your plan will be to pay only $484 worth of bills on the 1st and $484 on the 15th. Doing this will leave you with approximately the same amount of money in your checking account on each payday, after all your fixed expenses have been paid. Let's follow this example, assuming income is received bimonthly, on the 1st and 15th.

- Total fixed expenses = $968
- Total fixed expenses to be paid per payday = $484
- Total income received per month = $1,600
- Baseline income per payday = $800

Now comes the time to look at "balance." We've stressed the importance of balance in money matters, and here is where you will see its most pragmatic application.

Get a new sheet of paper and draw a line down the middle. Head one column 1st and one column 15th, and let's make some good decisions. We want you to determine on which payday each of your bills will be paid.

The factor that must remain constant is that only $484 (approximately) worth of bills will be paid on each date. Reviewing our list of fixed expenses from our example, we find that the rent is due on the 1st and it is $425. All mortgage companies will impose penalties on you for late payments of a mortgage, and landlords need to be paid on time because of their obligations to their own mortgage holders. The bottom line on rents and mortgages is that they are inflexible expenses. Their amounts and due dates can rarely be altered.

With that in mind, we have no choice but to designate the rent of $425 to be paid with the paycheck of the 1st. Because our plan was to pay only $484 worth of bills with each check, we can only pay approximately $60 of additional bills from this 1st paycheck. We could choose the electric bill, which we've listed at $60, or perhaps the phone and cable, which combine at $55, or gas and water which combine at $58. Any of these combinations would work well in our plan, but the problem becomes the due dates. We want to pay our bills on time, and maintain a current pay record as much as it is humanly possible.

3. If Necessary, Change the Due Dates on Bills.

But here's some good news. Many of the companies to which you pay your fixed-expense payments will gladly change your due date to fit into your plan. It is of primary importance to most companies to be paid once every thirty days; however, the date of that payment is merely a bookkeeping decision for them. It's true that a few hard-liners won't alter their bookkeeping arrangement to accommodate their customers, but it's also true that most of them will. So don't miss this opportunity. Arrange your pay plan and then call those companies whose due dates conflict and explain to them that you would like your due date changed because of your own pay schedule. The people you will talk to are people just like you, who are also trying to live comfortably on their own incomes and pay their own bills in a reasonably punctual way. Our clients report that they find most companies to be extremely cooperative and accommodating as soon as they realize that you're requesting this change so that you can pay them more punctually, more efficiently, and more reliably.

OK. Back to our chart. Suppose we've decided to pay the gas and water bills on the first and they total $58. The due date on the gas bill is the 10th, so there would be no need to change the date on it. If we write the check on the 1st and mail it, it should arrive in plenty of time to meet the 10th date. The water bill is a problem. Its due date is the 28th. We will need to call the water company and explain that we get paid on the 1st and that is when we'd like to mail the check, so if our due date could be changed from the 28th to the 10th, for example, we would remain current at all times, and the water department would have its money shortly after the 1st of each month.

Just for argument's sake, let's assume that the water department is not very accommodating to its customers and the management tells us the due date of the 28th is set in granite and could only changed by an amendment to the United States Constitution. You will run into people like this. Let's try first to work around them. Look at your other combinations. Perhaps, in the case of our example, the electric company might be more flexible or maybe the phone and cable companies would be helpful in this situation. If so, deal with them instead. The important thing is to pay only a total of $484; it doesn't matter which bills combine to make up that amount.

In the unfortunate event that all the companies you call are unwilling to help, then you must decide which bills are to be paid on the 1st, and stick to it. The companies are not going to complain too much, if at all, so long as they receive their payment once every thirty days. And if anyone does dare to call you and ask that you pay on one date instead of another, it's a perfect opportunity for you to ask them to call your employer and have your paycheck issued on a different date.

Of course, you need to avoid paying late charges, which some companies impose if you pay the bill late. So keep that in mind as you rearrange the payment dates on your bills.

Since most companies are very willing to help their customers, let's say that, in our example, we chose to pay the gas and water bill and got the water bill due date changed to the 10th.

Our new list will look like this:

1st	15th
$425 Rent (1st)	$ 60 Electric (22nd)
40 Gas (10th)	35 Phone (16th)
18 Water (10th)	20 Cable (18th)
	90 Insurance (25th)
	275 Loans (9th, 17th)
____	____5 Paper (30th)
$483	$485

Looking again at the due dates of the rest of the bills, we find that the electric bill is OK as it is with a due date of the 22nd. The phone will need to be moved a few days because our payment probably won't get there in one day. Cable should be fine, and insurance will present no problems. The car loan will need to be changed and so will the student loan, but the newspaper is fine.

For most of these companies, changing a due date is as simple as going to the computer and making the change. You may also find how willing people are to help you when they see you're doing all you can, and that in helping you, they will be contributing to their own well-being. You'll be paying your bills on a regular basis and in an efficient manner.

4. Pay Your Bills Only on Your Payday, and Not Any Other Time.

The most commonly asked question in a counseling session, once we've arranged the client's plan, is this: "You mean I shouldn't pay these other bills before the 15th even if they come in?" The answer is emphatically "No!"

The reason we've divided these fixed expenses is to give you some balance and some constancy, by leaving you with the same amount of money to spend out of each paycheck. You will get used to having this amount of money, and will feel comfortable with it. The "boom or bust" pattern, which gives us all an uncomfortable, insecure, feeling, will be eliminated.

The key words then for fixed expenses are: *reducing, levelizing,* and *timing.*

So now let's look at that regular income. Our example showed a monthly income of $1,600, paid to the client in two paychecks of $800 each, one on the 1st and one on the 15th. Our chart now looks like this:

	1st	15th
Income	$800	$800
Fixed Expenses	- 483	- 485
Controllable Expenses	$317	$315

This will give you a clear figure to keep in mind of exactly how much money you will have to spend on your controllable expenses in order to remain solvent. The following chapter on *controllable expenses* will go into great detail, explaining which expenses fall into that category and how to handle them.

Timing—When You Are Paid Monthly, Weekly, or Biweekly

Most people manage their bills better if they receive their paychecks twice a month on the same dates every month (such as the 1st and the 15th). However, if you receive your paychecks on a different pay schedule, it is extremely unlikely that your employer will be willing or able to change the way in which you are paid to accommodate an easier plan. Being paid monthly, weekly, or biweekly may require a little more pre-arranging on your part before settling on a plan, but once you have it in place, it will work equally well.

If You Are Paid Monthly

If you are paid monthly, you will write your checks once a month. Most of the due dates will not matter. If you are paid on the last day of each month, you will simply write out all the checks for your fixed expenses for that month whether or not you have the bills. Because you will have levelized as many bills as possible, you will have an accurate idea of the amount of each bill you'll be receiving. And on the ones that cannot be levelized, your power to estimate will still be quite good. For instance, the phone bill is not one that any of us can levelize, but we can rely on the same amount each month for the basic service we've selected. Suppose you know your basic phone service to be $29 per month. When you receive your paycheck on the last day of the month, write out all your bills including the $29, which you know will go to the phone company. When the phone bill arrives, perhaps on the 18th of the month, you will have the check for $29 ready and you can write an additional check at that time to cover whatever small difference you couldn't account for (such as a long distance call). If your long-distance bill is consistently more than $100 per month, then write your check for $100 and write a second check for the difference. Tailor your plan to fit your lifestyle.

If You Are Paid Weekly

If you are paid once a week, the principle is the same, but it is a little more difficult to organize your payments. You will receive four checks a month for eight months out of the year, and an extra check for four months because of months with five paydays. You should work your plan based on receiving four checks per month as baseline monthly income and should treat the fifth check as acceleration income. All fixed expenses, of course, will be paid out of baseline monthly income.

The easiest way to look at this will be to think of your checks as checks Nos. 1, 2, 3, and 4. For example, check No. 1 will be the first check received in a month, check No. 2 will be the second. You will pay bills four times a month, each time you receive your check. So, you need to divide your fixed-expense bills into four lists, one list to be paid with check No. 1, one list to be paid with check No. 2, etc.

You will have two problems: (1) due dates, and (2) the rent or mortgage. The due dates may need to be altered for your convenience, and the rent or mortgage will more than likely be too large to be paid out of any one check. So you need to divide your rent/mortgage payment into two halves and pay half out of check No. 3 and half out of check No. 4. When it's time to pay your rent/mortgage, mail both checks.

In the example we used before, our client had a monthly take-home pay of $1,600, so her weekly take-home pay would have been $370 per week. ($1,600 x 12 months = $19,200; $19,200 divided by 52 weeks = $370) Her fixed expense bills were $968 per month, and one-fourth of that ($242) needed to be paid each week.

Paying attention to each due date, she divided her bills as follows:

Check No. 1

Income	$370	
Car loan		$175 due 9th
Water		18 due 10th
Gas		40 due 10th
Insurance		10 due 25th (partial pmt)
Total expenses	- 243	
Money Left	$127	

Check No. 2

Income	$370	
Student loan		$100 due 17th
Cable		20 due 18th
Phone		35 due 16th
Electric		60 due 22nd
Newspaper		5 due 30th
Insurance		20 due 25th (partial pmt)
Total expenses	- 240	
Money left	$130	

Check No. 3

Income	$370	
Rent 1/2		$213 due 1st
Insurance		__30 due 25th (partial pmt)
Total expenses	- 243	
Money left	$127	

Check No. 4

Income	$370	
Rent 1/2		$212 due 1st
Insurance		__30 due 25th*
Total expenses	- 242	
Money left	$128	

What will be apparent to you by now is that all the due dates will be OK as they are except for the insurance. Your last check will arrive too late to make the due date of the 25th, but one phone call will probably take care of that.

If You Are Paid Biweekly

If you are paid every other week, you will pay bills only twice a month. Check No. 1 will be the check you receive between the 1st and the 14th of the month, and check No. 2 will be the second check you receive later in the month. Pay your rent or house payment with check No. 2, and then arrange payment of your other bills based on the money left from your baseline monthly income, which should remain constant.

---

* Write the insurance checks weekly but do not mail them until you have written the final check in Week 4.

Twice a year, you will receive three checks in one month. The third check should be used as acceleration money. Divide the payment of your bills between checks No. 1 and No. 2 only.

The major difficulty in being paid every other week is, again, the due dates. It is impractical and inconsiderate to continue changing due dates with your various creditors, so rearranging *your* plan more frequently is probably more realistic. Just remember a few things:

- You've levelized each bill, and you know the basic amount to be paid.
- You will only pay a certain dollar amount of total fixed expenses each time you write checks.
- You will always try to leave yourself approximately the same amount of "money left" after paying your bills.

Be aware that it is a little more difficult to manage a system when you are paid every other week, and that you will have to give extra attention to your bills and to your plan. But revising your plan will not be difficult. After such a close examination of your financial condition, you will become well acquainted with your personal money management. So whatever your income and expense schedule turns out to be, you will begin to see how much control you can have over something that previously may have seemed baffling.

Conclusion

By now you should have your own charts completed, indicating the following:

- which expenses are your fixed expenses
- how much each one is
- the due dates of each or whether those due dates need to be changed for your own benefit
- the total of the fixed expenses

By dividing and scheduling your bill payments to match your pay schedules, you now have figured out how much money is left over for controllable expenses, once you've paid all the fixed expenses.

Please note here that you still have not determined the amount of your savings payment. Keep that in mind, and be aware that your plan will need to be adjusted later to accommodate this decision; but at this point, you haven't enough information with which to make a good decision.

The benefits of establishing a plan for these fixed expenses are as follows:

- You get to see immediately if you're living beyond your means in terms of basic living expenses.
- You review your present fixed expenses and determine the validity of each one. This is a perfect opportunity to make changes if needed.
- You can make your own decisions as to how and when you pay these bills. You make an arrangement that suits your financial best interest.

According to our rule of thumb that fixed expenses should total no more than 65 percent of regular income, our example is in the ballpark: 65% of $1,600 = $1,040, with fixed expenses totalling $968.

If fixed expenses had totalled $1,450, with income of only $1,600, our client would have had to make some hard decisions about whether to continue living where she was living, whether to keep cable service or keep the car, or which inordinately high expense to eliminate.

Whatever your chart looks like, be pleased with it. If the numbers work out well, you have gained the knowledge that your basic expenses are in line with your income. If the numbers work out "not well," at least you understand the exact nature of the financial stress you may have only vaguely defined before. Then you have gained the knowledge of what must be changed in order to make the best possible choice for yourself regarding your financial condition.

Whatever the financial outcome, don't lose sight of the fact that your power of choice is a direct result of establishing and maintaining balance. Don't allow any other person, company or organization to make your decisions for you. Act in your own best interest and with your own self-empowerment in mind. Don't beat yourself up emotionally if the numbers on your chart don't work out well. Take it as an opportunity to change your life for the better. You'll feel good about yourself, and many of the stresses that living beyond your means can cause will evaporate.

Controllable Expenses

At this point, you have (1) determined your income, and (2) levelized your fixed expenses and assigned each of them to one of your paychecks. Your next step is to work on what we call *controllable expenses*. First, we will define controllable expenses. Second, we will show you how to examine your past controllable expenses. Third, we will show you how to change your thinking about these expenses to gain control of them. Finally, we will show you how to control your controllables.

Because you have levelized your fixed expenses and assigned them to paychecks, the good news is that you now know exactly how much money you have in each paycheck to spend on controllable expenses. It may be $50 or $3,000, but it is yours to spend exactly as you choose.

The bad news is that that amount of money is *all* you have to spend. This may be dismaying to you, or it may be OK. But it is a fact. If you spend more than that amount, you are going into debt. No one can consistently, every month, go into debt and survive financially. You will fall behind on your obligations, have your credit lines shut off, sink into insolvency, and perhaps be forced to claim bankruptcy. That is an undesirable outcome, so your job now is to allocate this specific sum of money among your controllable expenses in the way that brings you the greatest satisfaction, without spending more than that amount of money.

What are Controllable Expenses?

Controllable expenses are expenses that you control totally or to a great degree, which you willingly and knowingly incur and which you could choose not to incur. Controllable expenses are expenses other than fixed expenses and unusual expenses, such as auto or house-repair expenses. (These large, extraordinary expenses will be covered by your savings. See Chapter 6 on savings.)

The most common controllable expenses are

- food (all food, not just groceries for the house. Included in this group would be all meals eaten in restaurants, all fast food, all snacks, such as candy and ice cream, and all drinks.)
- house maintenance (cleaning expenses, yard care, routine maintenance such as exterminators)
- transportation (gasoline, parking, and public transportation)
- entertainment (movies, video rentals, bowling, trips, hobbies, vacations)
- credit cards (Visa, MasterCard, American Express)
- charge cards (department stores, catalogs)

- charitable contributions
- addictions (liquor, drugs, smoking, gambling)
- taking-care-of-me expense (personal care, clothes, grooming, medical, health)
- child-rearing expenses (day-care, education, allowance, clothing, medical)

Examine Your Past Controllable Expenses

The best way to begin deciding how to allocate your money among possible controllable expenses is to look at what you have been spending your money on. Look at three months' expenses. Use your checkbook record or canceled checks and credit and charge card statements to see what you have been spending. If you use cash entirely, you will not have a good record of your expenditures. You will have to develop a record over one or two months by purchasing a small notebook and writing down your cash expenditures (and keeping a record of money orders you may have purchased), or by writing checks for nearly all of your purchases. Make a chart of your controllable expenditures, as follows:

	Month 1	**Month 2**	**Month 3**
Food			
grocery			
restaurant			
House maintenance			
Transportation			
Entertainment			
Credit Card Payments			
Charge Card Payments			
Charitable Contributions			
Addictions			
Personal Care			

	Month 1	**Month 2**	**Month 3**
Child-Rearing			
day care			
health			
school			
allowance			
clothes			
other			
Other (itemize)			

After you have made your list, think about what you are spending your money on. Do you feel good about your allocation of money, or are there some obvious imbalances? Are you spending $2,000 a month on your child and nothing for your personal care? Are your credit and charge card payments crippling you? Don't do a major analysis at this point, just let yourself become aware of the way you have been spending your money.

Finally, add up your controllable expenses for each month. Are they less or more than the amount that remains out of each paycheck for controllable expenses? *Be aware of whether your spending practices are getting you into debt.* To continue the example from Chapter 4, let's look at the following chart:

Income	$1600 per month
Fixed expenses	- 968 per month
Controllable expenses	$ 632 for controllables

Major Items of Controllable Expense

Now let's look at some of the major items of controllable expenses more closely to see how you can make them truly controllable.

Food

Because food is a basic necessity of life, you may wonder why we put it in the list of controllable expenses rather than fixed expenses. Food is a fascinating topic. It can be many things simultaneously. It is definitely a basic necessity, it can frequently be entertainment or a big part of entertainment, and it is sometimes an addiction. The reason we put it in controllable expenses is that it cannot be levelized. It is an emotional topic which people handle in various ways, and few people actually go to the grocery store with calculator in hand, armed with the magic budget figure they will not exceed no matter what. On the emotional side, most of us avoid going shopping when we feel hungry for fear we'll buy everything in sight. If we could just set a food figure of, say, $100 per week, and not worry about exceeding it, going to the grocery store would never present a problem for anyone. But, in fact, grocery purchases can be a real budget buster.

We have some suggestions. First, except for the occasional milk run between paydays, go shopping only on paydays. Purchase all of your groceries in one major shopping trip. If you eat mostly fresh fruits and vegetables and prefer to shop for these daily, put aside your grocery money each time you are paid. Next, shop with awareness. If your priorities center around always having plenty of food in the house, but you don't care to eat much in restaurants, then concentrate your efforts on spending your controllable money at the grocery store. If your priorities center around a hobby and it's OK with you to have the cupboards empty, then go with that. The important goal with this, as with other expenses, is that you not pay for what you don't need or want, and that you spend money to coincide with your needs and desires.

House Maintenance

This category includes cleaning supplies and the other routine expenses of maintaining your house or apartment, including the cost of a cleaning service and yard care, if you employ people to do this work. It does not include the occasional expensive household repairs and major maintenance such as painting. If you have a cleaning or yard person, you could, of course, reduce your monthly expenses by cleaning your own house or mowing your own yard, but if you have chosen to pay a cleaning or yard person, these expenditures are probably a priority for you. Do think, however, about whether you would be willing to clean your own house if it gave you an extra $100 or more a month to spend on other things. Make a choice.

Transportation

This category includes the cost of gasoline for your car, parking, and public transportation. Car insurance and car payments are included in fixed expenses and should not be included here. We recommend that you levelize and control your gasoline expenses by using a gasoline credit card and paying this expense once a month, on the payday you select. If you use public transportation daily, a monthly rider's card may be available from your public transit authority which would allow you to travel without limit on public transportation for a single monthly fee. This will save you money, so you should plan to purchase a monthly rider's card out of the same paycheck each month.

Without a driver's license, it can sometimes be difficult to obtain access to services. One of our clients had difficulty obtaining a rider's card because she had no picture ID. The only recommendation we could think of was that she obtain a passport. Although the primary use of passports is for travel out of the country, they also serve very well for identification because they have your photograph, signature, and social security number, and are very official. The cost is $65 for a passport, which is valid for ten years. You also have to furnish a passport photograph which costs $7 to $10 in our town. Although that may seem like a high cost, it is less than the charge for a driver's license in some states. To apply for a passport, get in touch with your post office.

You can save some money on transportation by scheduling all of your errands for the same day once a week or once every other week. You can also save money by driving a compact car rather than a large gas-guzzler. Still it probably would not make economic sense to buy a new car just to save money on gasoline. You can buy a lot of gasoline for the amount of a car payment. Another way of saving money without buying a new car is car-pooling to work and other places. A little organization on transportation can result in significant savings without a great loss of convenience.

Another major transportation expense in some cities is parking. In smaller cities, you will typically pay from $20 to $50 per month for parking, and in larger cities, the cost can be several times that amount. If you are looking for a job, you should take into account whether your employer will pay for your parking. If not, consider it a reduction in salary. The lower paying job that provides parking and other benefits may actually leave you with more money in your pocket than the higher paying job that leaves many of the expenses up to you. If your employer does not pay for parking, and the expense is unreasonably high, consider using public transportation or car-pooling to reduce your transportation expense.

Entertainment

For the record, before you start equating a money plan with deprivation (talking about entertainment is where this usually happens), we want to make it clear that everyone needs and deserves some entertainment. We would never leave entertainment out of this plan. But we do want to emphasize that entertainment that puts you deeper and deeper into debt will not be entertaining for too long. So, be balanced and reasonable. At this point in your life you might be able to go the movies without a second thought, but probably you can't just fly off to Paris or London. If a trip to Paris or London is on the top of your list, then you will gear your plan to accommodate such a trip down the line. But, for the most part, if you're just beginning your plan, you need to recognize that entertainment expenses should be within the reasonable financial limits that you set. Staying within your own limits will make you feel comfortable, unstressed, and proud of your accomplishment.

If you have a regular entertainment activity that means a lot to you, don't give it up unless you absolutely have to. One client, whose fixed expenses were unpleasantly high in relation to her income, spent more than $60 a month at her tennis club. That money would have helped a lot to make the rest of her plan work. But she loved tennis, and it was her primary recreational activity. She decided that the tennis club expenses would not be eliminated unless there was absolutely no other way for her to meet her fixed obligations. By using some of the other techniques described in this book, she was able to keep her tennis club membership. So be very reluctant to give up entertainment that you love. It's a last resort. Don't punish yourself for not having handled your money quite so well as you think you should have. Punishment is not the goal—taking care of yourself is.

Credit and Charge Cards

Credit and charge-card debt have the American public in a half-Nelson, and everyone is yelling "Uncle!" Credit and charge-card payments for items purchased some time ago are expense items that all of us would like to eliminate from our list of controllable expenses. Because you have already enjoyed the purchases, there is no satisfaction in paying for them over a long period of time. It feels like throwing money away when we write those monthly checks.

Do you feel trapped by debt? There is no reason to alter your spending habits if they cause you no stress; but if you are feeling trapped or overwhelmed by credit-card debt, then exercise your power of choice: choose to do something to alleviate your stress.

Act in your own best interest. Your situation, whatever it is, does not require drastic measures unless you feel it does. We are not making the point that credit cards, charge cards, department stores or catalog shopping are all potential evils. They are all neutral. You decide whether they are good for you or bad for you, and make your decisions based on that. It is wise to make sure that your actions are as closely aligned with your best interest as possible. The extent to which that alignment is off is the extent to which you will feel uncomfortable and under stress.

Be honest with yourself. Some people can carry a Visa in their wallet for years for the purpose of emergency credit (a very valid reason) and are never even tempted to use it otherwise. Other cards go in and out of wallets so frequently that the magnetic strip on the back gets worn off.

Consider paying off your credit and charge cards entirely. Short of going bankrupt, the only way to eliminate this monthly expense is by paying it off. You can do it, and in the course of one, two, or three years this controllable expense can be reduced, then eliminated from your list.

Put your credit cards away. If you've had enough of paying on your Visa, then we suggest that you remove the card from your wallet, place it in your desk drawer, make the decision to stop using it, and list it in your fixed expenses as a regular monthly payment until the balance is paid down to zero, just as you do with loans.

How do you feel about leaving your cards in the drawer? If you are unable to put it in the desk drawer because you get chest pains whenever you think that it is not in your wallet, then we suggest you read Chapter 10 on addictions (pay close attention to the "spending" section) and congratulate yourself on finding one of the possible causes of your financial stress.

What about emergencies? We had one client who told us that she wanted to stop using her Visa but didn't want to leave it in the desk drawer for fear she might encounter an emergency and would need the card. She did, however, make the decision to stop using the card and changed the categorization of the Visa payment to fixed expenses with the intent to eventually pay off the balance completely.

Each month she would come back to see us, and the balance would be higher and higher. Apparently, her definition of emergency was different from ours—we thought she meant she'd use it if the car broke down. What she actually meant was if a blouse went on sale. Leaving the Visa in the desk drawer turned out to be a choice she felt she had to make.

Catalog shopping. One of our clients disliked shopping so much she rarely went to the store. Her downfall, however, was catalogs. She quickly ended up on every catalog mailing list and would regularly receive dozens of catalogs, which advertised everything from clothes to furniture to outdoor supplies. You name it, she had a catalog that sold it. There was always something in each catalog that struck her or that she felt she might be able to use. She felt it was becoming a real problem for her, so, at first, she tried to simply throw out the catalogs when they arrived. She soon found that that didn't work, and that she would either retrieve them from the trash or read them on the way to the garbage. Finally, she contacted each catalog company and requested that her name be taken off the mailing list.

How to get what you want without charging. One reason people use credit and charge cards is the "have to have it now" syndrome. If you use credit, you can have something now and pay for it later. We do not believe people need to have things now, but we do believe people need to take steps now to assure themselves that, eventually, they will have what they want. Rather than using credit, you can save money out of your income to purchase an item that one month's expenditure cannot cover.

Suppose the month is March, and you have been annoyed all winter that you did not have an attractive dress coat to wear with your good clothes. You believe you can buy what you want for no more than $400. Start putting aside $40 a month for your coat, either in savings or in an envelope. In ten months, you will have enough to buy the coat. If you can only earmark $20 a month for a coat, it will take 20 months to save $400. But remember, coats go on sale in December or January, so you may be able to pick up a bargain by the middle of next winter. In any event, you will know that at some time, not too far off, you will have a nice dress coat and absolutely no new debt. We don't actually need to have everything we want right this minute to feel good and in control; often, just taking steps that assure us we will have what we want fairly soon will be equally satisfying.

Paying cash may in some circumstances save you money. You may be able to obtain a lower price than the credit price. This is particularly true for large appliances and new and used cars. Cash may give you bargaining power that credit does not.

Earn interest on your money instead of paying interest. Consider this. Twenty months is almost two years. If $20 is all you can afford per month, and you choose to charge the coat, then it will take you almost two years to pay off that bill, and you'll be accruing interest all along the way. By the time you're finished, that coat will have cost you about $550. If you save the money in the bank, interest will be paid *to you* all along the way. You will have $400 about a month-and-a-half sooner than if your money did not earn interest. Make your decision with this awareness.

Charitable Contributions

When we began counseling, we never imagined that charitable contributions would present a problem. And, in truth, we found that they either present no problem or a serious problem. Many clients simply chose not to make any charitable contributions, and so the item was never a component of their finances. But of the clients who did choose to contribute, very few did so in a reasonable manner in relation to their income.

We actually had clients who were two months behind on some of their fixed expenses (electric, gas, water bills), yet contributed heavily to charities without fail. If it is your desire to contribute to a charity on a regular basis, then review your income and your fixed expenses, determine the amount of money you have left for controllable items, and then make a decision.

If you find that you cannot meet your fixed expenses and yet feel an overwhelming need to continue to contribute to a particular charity, there is probably an emotional component to your decision. This would be a good opportunity to examine your motivation behind proceeding with a course of action that is not in your financial best interest.

Addictions

Become aware of the effect an addiction may have on your financial plan. We will look extensively at addictions in Chapter 10. However, we wish to emphasize that addictions are not controllable expenses until the addictions themselves are controlled. They are a major cause of why the best plans fail. The obvious financial drain of a drug, alcohol or gambling addiction has made for many a gruesome story. We hear and read heartwrenching stories, which describe families losing their homes or the provider of the family losing the job that supplied the main income, because of addictions they were unable to overcome. Keep in mind that no plan will succeed if you have an addiction or if your partner has an addiction that is allowed to impair the household finances. We urge you to take care of that problem first. Seek the help of a professional counselor and let ending the addiction (if it is your addiction) or becoming detached from the addiction (if it is your partner's) be your first step toward going from paychecks to power.

The Seeking-Approval Expense

What is the *seeking-approval expense?* We spoke briefly about the seeking-approval expense in the introduction, and it will be discussed in depth in the chapter on addictions, but let's look at it in relation to controllable money. We define the seeking-approval expense as an expense incurred to obtain the approval of others.

This can be anything from continually giving your child spending money that you can't spare, to spending thousands of dollars landscaping your yard so that neighbors won't look disapprovingly at it as they drive by, or to making inappropriately large contributions to employer-supported charities in order to maintain a certain status. One client could not maintain a rational financial plan because he spent a great deal of money on clothes. He felt compelled to do that because he believed he had a high-profile job that demanded a certain image. He did, in fact, present the image of a very well-dressed, corporate executive. Sadly, though, that image was a house of cards. His financial practices were a balancing act that could not be maintained forever.

Follow your heart. At this point, we must confess to a strong prejudice. We believe that the happiest people are those who have given up seeking the approval of others in favor of following the dictates of their own hearts. There is nothing so imprisoning as the need for approval. It overshadows every decision and never allows your real desires to see the light of day. Be more caring of yourself than that. Give your *self*—your *true self*—a chance to breathe—a chance to make her real feelings known. Treat yourself with respect and with honor.

If you have spent money you really didn't have or really didn't want to spend in order to gain the approval of someone else, remember that the past is the past. Don't chastise yourself. But turn over a new leaf! Recognize that if your desire to gain others' approval is so great you would destroy yourself financially, the seeking-approval expense is an issue you will have to deal with directly in order to get free of it. And you will want to get free of it!

The Taking-Care-of-Me Expense

What is the *taking-care-of-me expense?* We suggest that, if you find you have an addiction or are subject to the seeking-approval expense, you replace these expenditures with what we call the taking-care-of-me expense. This expense could become your most crucial and important controllable expense.

Think about what you need to spend in order to take proper care of yourself. You have medical and dental needs, therapy or counseling, hair care, make-up, lotions and perfumes, clothes and accessories, and health maintenance expenses, such as exercise classes or health club dues. It can cost a lot of money to take lavish, thorough care of yourself. But if you do not plan to pay proper attention to these expenses, your plan will not work as well. If your hair is overgrown, you let yourself get out of shape, or you stop therapy or do not start it because of the expense, you will feel bad about yourself and bad about your plan.

Maintain balance. On the other hand, if you overspend compulsively on clothes and so forth, your plan will also be disrupted. What you are seeking here are two things: (1) identifying what will actually make you feel better inside versus expenses made to impress other people or satisfy the nagging voice within you that tells you how imperfect you are; and (2) maintaining balance in this as in all other areas of your life.

Do you neglect your needs? If you have not been paying enough attention to your own needs, we want you to make a resolution. Allocate a certain amount of money out of your next paycheck to do something for yourself. Even if you can only allocate $5, do allocate that amount. Think about what you can do for yourself for that amount of money, and when your paycheck arrives, fulfill your resolution to yourself and spend that money taking care of you. Do this each and every paycheck without fail. This will give you a good feeling about yourself and your plan and will help you to overcome any obstacles you may face from time to time.

Start now to take care of yourself. If, because of obligations you have made in the past, you simply do not have the money to take excellent care of yourself, one of your primary goals will be to get into a position where you can do this. And start doing what you can do right now.

Examine the expenses you now have. First, take a look at the taking-care-of-me expenses you have right now. Do you belong to a health club you do not use? If so, you probably joined it either for the status of belonging to that particular club (the seeking-approval expense) or in order to quiet that nagging inner voice.

Discover what you really love. Instead of whipping yourself into a frenzy of resolution to start using the health club, sit quietly and think about active hobbies and occupations you think you might really enjoy. Think about what you've enjoyed in the past. Did you like square dancing as a child? Did you used to love to ride your bike? Does it feel good when you stretch? Do you like the smell of the earth and the feel of sunshine on your body? Get into your body and visualize what feels good to it.

Do you enjoy doing things in groups or by yourself? Do you enjoy the excitement of competition, or do you find it distressing? Try to get to know yourself and what feels good physically and emotionally.

One of our clients joined a square dancing group. Another returned to her old love of gardening. One found some yoga classes. One, a licensed masseuse, went back to doing massage for the physical exercise and emotional satisfaction, as well as a little extra money. One client simply started going on longer walks with her dog.

All of these activities were less expensive than a typical health club. If you love your health club and go often, keep it up by all means. But if it's not what you really want to do, drop it, even if you have to forfeit a membership fee. And please, use the money you save from that to really take care of yourself.

Spend your money to make yourself feel the best. Let's say you've dropped your health club and have the extra $30 a month. How can you spend that money to give yourself the best feeling inside? Personally, we believe that a good haircut is absolutely essential to a satisfactory quality of life, and ranked close behind that is having our favorite perfume. If those items were already taken care of, we would go down our list looking for the thing (or combination of things) that we could buy or do with our $30 that would make us feel the best. It might be getting our teeth cleaned, getting an overdue medical check-up, yoga or dance classes. It might be a new self-help book. But we'd definitely try to get the most for our money.

Clothing Expense

Let's talk about clothes. Clothes are a very tricky subject. On the one hand, we all know how important it is to present a good image; on the other hand, they are very expensive. On the third hand (we have four between us, so why not?) it is hard to feel good if you aren't dressed in clothes you enjoy that are appropriate to your activities.

Clothes and balance. Most of our clients are seriously out of balance on the subject of clothes. They can be divided into two groups: (1) those who spend the electric bill money on clothes; and (2) those who never have anything to wear that they feel good about. One client's only coat was a ratty, ragged old thing she avoided wearing even on the coldest days. One client had expensive business clothes but nothing to wear to a party or for leisure activities. None of these approaches is balanced. While we normally abhor rules, we have a few simple rules for clothes.

- Don't spend any fixed-expenses money on clothes.
- Have at least one thing you enjoy wearing for every activity you engage in.
- Have warm clothes for the winter and cool clothes for the summer.
- Never buy anything that doesn't fit comfortably when you buy it.

Buy what you need gradually, within your income. Decide how much you can afford to spend on clothes each month. If you need clothes, decide what you need the most, and use your money to buy that. Then buy the next thing on your list, and so on. Over time, you should have a nice wardrobe of clothes you enjoy wearing.

Many of you may want new clothes, but the numbers of your personal finances just don't work out in your favor. If this is the case, don't be discouraged. Realize that, beginning now with your new plan, you will be laying the groundwork needed to pay off your debts and get yourself in a position where purchasing clothes will not be a financial hardship for you.

Clothes as gifts. Luckily, clothes are frequently given as gifts. If friends or family ask you what you want for Christmas or for your birthday, don't hesitate to specify exactly what you would like to have. It's not rude. These people love you, and they want you to have something you really want. So be specific! Your wardrobe will improve even faster.

Do you buy clothes compulsively? If you're the type who "buys clothes with the electric bill money" (in other words, uses money that should pay fixed expenses), you almost certainly have plenty to wear. Your problem is going to be resisting the compulsion to spend more on clothes than you actually can afford to spend. We discuss the spending addiction in Chapter 10. For now, we'll just mention that the more genuine care you take of yourself—the more you do things that make you feel good inside—the less you will feel the compulsion to wildly spend and buy.

The Child-Rearing Expense

We love our children, and we want them to have a good life now and in the future. Their needs and desires are enormous, and most mothers want to give their children not only what they need but what they want. Meeting the needs and desires of your children can be the biggest item in your controllable expenses.

Examine your child-rearing expenses from the perpective of balance. Take a long, hard look at your child-rearing expenses. There may be many ways you can and should cut these expenses without impairing your child's happiness or opportunities in life. In fact, if you are out of balance in how you handle child-rearing expenses, your child will benefit greatly from your beginning to operate in a realistic, balanced way.

What's good for your finances is good for your children. One of our clients lavished money on his teenage son. He sent him to an expensive private school in a part of the country where it was common for middle-class and upper-middle-class families to send their children to public school, bought name-brand clothes at an expensive department store, and gave the boy $40 or $50 nearly every week to go "malling." While he had a good income, it wasn't that good. Worse than the effect these practices were having on his finances was the effect they were having on his son, who was being reared with no idea of how to earn or manage money and with the notion that a primary goal in life was to have enough money and material things to impress his peers.

Another client, after financial counseling and a lot of soul-searching, took a very active position with her son regarding money. She explained to him what her financial situation was and why she really could not afford to do some things she had done in the past, such as sending him to camp. She researched alternative activities available in the community at much lower cost. She took him out of private school, which he had not wanted to attend, and selected a public school he did want to attend, one she believed would offer a good education.

More drastically (from a teenager's point of view), she explained to him that, as he was fourteen, he would need to earn his own spending money by working for neighbors on their lawns, caring for pets, and doing other jobs for which, nowadays, there are not nearly enough willing teenagers. Then she totally eliminated his allowance. He went through three or four weeks of poverty before seeking employment, and from then on felt the independence and satisfaction that comes from earning one's own money.

The only problem our client had with her actions was that she could no longer use as discipline the threat of cutting off his allowance, but this turned out to be positive as well. She was forced to bargain and negotiate a great deal more. She and her son found that this changed economic relationship caused them to regard each other with considerably more respect.

Pressure from children. Some children will threaten dire consequences if you refuse to buy them what they want. They will state that, if they cannot have the $120, air-powered tennis shoes that "all the other kids have," their lives will no longer be worth living. They will commit suicide, or go on drugs, and it will be all your fault. You can be a great help to your child when a crisis like this arises, by helping him/her to separate emotional happiness or unhappiness from the desire to acquire a specific material item. There is no doubt that your child feels a great deal of stress. If your child states an intent to commit suicide or use drugs, you should take this very seriously and enroll the child in a counseling group. But you should tell the child that you do not believe that having the tennis shoes will reduce his suicidal tendencies, so you are not going to purchase them. Give him your blessing to go out and find work to earn the $120.

What if they say they'll go live with Dad? Another common threat, if you're divorced, is that they'll go live with their dads. Your child may actually have an emotional need to spend more time with his or her father. So, unless your ex-husband is a child molester or abusive in other ways, take this possibility seriously and tell the child you will consider it and talk to his father about it. If you decide to allow your child to live with his father, don't allow yourself to feel bad about it. Your child may be focusing verbally on the economic advantages of living with dad, but the chances are good that the unspoken emotional needs are legitimate, and that you would be doing your child a favor by honoring the child's desire.

College. College can be unbelievably costly. Use balance with regard to these expenses as well. Put your energy into investigating the availability of grants and scholarships and do a careful economic comparison of several schools you are considering. Also, you and your college student can ask yourselves some hard questions: Can he or she handle a part-time job? Can the student afford the added expense of a fraternity or sorority, and do the benefits outweigh the cost? Can living off-campus or at home make college affordable when otherwise it might not be? Can your child's interests and abilities be better served by a community or state college than by a more expensive private school?

Does it make good economic sense to take your child out of private school in the lower grades in order to be financially able to send him or her to college later? Finally, do you owe your child the most expensive education, or any college education, if it will ruin you financially? We believe that what you do owe your child is your attention and energy and a financial investment that is reasonable in light of your other obligations.

A friend of ours likes to tell the story of his college education. His parents sent him to an expensive private college. He left after one year, then worked for several years. He realized that he really needed and wanted a college education, and went back to his father. His father explained that the parents could not contribute any more to his education, as they needed to save for their own retirement. Our friend worked his way through college, and was very proud of that fact all the years thereafter. He felt his father had actually done him a favor by refusing to subsidize him any more and by treating him as an autonomous adult. Furthermore, he had the comfort of knowing that his parents had provided well for their own retirement, and that he would not have to contribute financially to their support in later years.

Not every child will view the lack of college money as positively as our friend did. However, the belief that "the absence of financial support equals failure, and the presence of financial support equals success," is a false one. This story demonstrates that spending less does not guarantee disaster, and, in fact, may have a positive result.

Controlling Your Controllables

You have taken a look at what you typically spend on controllables and we have examined attitudes that can make them more controllable. Now is the time for you to exercise your power of choice. Using the same chart as shown on pages 73 and 74, make a new list of what you want your controllables to be. If you have decided to stop using your credit cards, eliminate that item from your list of controllables and move it to fixed expenses. Then, of course, you will have to reduce the amount of controllable money you have, because your fixed expenses will increase by the amount of your credit card payments. If there are any items of controllable expense that you wish to cut, make those adjustments. Work with your chart by trying to stay in balance. Keep within the amount of money you have to spend. Get the maximum amount of satisfaction out of your spending.

Honor your passions. If gourmet cooking is your passion, you will want to acknowledge that and spend a good portion of your money on food. If going to the movies is an activity you can't live without, then spending your money there will be very worthwhile to you. If the contributions you make to your favorite charity are most important in your life, then by all means, continue to write those checks and never give them a second thought.

Spending more than you have = stress. A little addition and subtraction will enable you to know exactly how much money you have to play with. Spending more than that amount will cause you stress because it will almost certainly send you into insolvency and perhaps into bankruptcy. Staying within the limits of your funds will keep you solvent, but if your money is being spent in a way that is not pleasing to you, then your stress will still be high.

Learn to feel powerful. As you can probably tell, the real problem in controllable expenses arises when you are spending money in a way that is not satisfying to you, and yet you feel powerless to stop it. This is a problem for two reasons: (1) You begin to feel that you're throwing your hard-earned money away; and (2) You begin to feel stupid, powerless, vulnerable, and trapped.

Permit yourself to be flexible, at least in your imagination. If you are really short of money, and are paying $300 a month for your child's school, visualize what your life and your child's life would be like if you moved him/her to a public school or a less expensive private school. If your food expenses are high and you frequently eat out, imagine cooking more meals at home. Keep imagining and playing with your expenses until you have the best plan for you, and don't be surprised if you modify your plan several times before settling on one that meets your needs. Then, execute your plan with courage, discipline, and personal power.

Reward yourself. As you figure out your controllables for the next paycheck, try to build in a little reward for yourself. You have looked at your income, and you may have made some adjustments in the deductions from your paycheck to give you more spending money. You have levelized your fixed expenses, and planned your controllables. Most clients find at this point that they actually have a little extra money. If that is true for you, reward yourself. Spend a little money on the thing that will give you the most satisfaction. One couple we counseled found they had $100 extra at this point in their planning. She decided to spend her $50 on a body wave, and he decided to spend his $50 on sports equipment.

Conclusion

Let's now follow our example with the new hypothetical figures for controllable expenses.

Monthly income		$ 1600
Less fixed expenses		
Rent	$425	
Electric	60	
Gas	40	
Water	18	
Phone	35	
Cable	20	
Insurance	90	
Loans	275	
Newspaper	5	
Savings	____*	
Subtotal		− 632

---

* not yet determined

Less controllables

Food	$250
House maintenance	15
Transportation	45
Entertainment	60
Credit Cards	35
Charge Cards	0
Charitable contributions	18
Addictions (smoking)	30
Clothing	30
Beauty shop	20

Subtotal   – 503

Money left $ 129

Make a list for yourself, and practice spending within your plan for several pay periods. Adjust your plan if you discover a different spending pattern is appropriate. Pay particular attention to your feelings during this crucial time, doing everything you can to avoid feeling deprived. Treat yourself especially well. After a few months, you will become very comfortable with your knowledge of how much you have to spend on controllables, and you will be able to relax and still be fully in control. This is when your plan really starts to work and when you will begin to feel truly powerful. Remember your plan will actually work faster and better than you thought, thanks to acceleration income and other factors that will be discussed in the following chapters.

Tools for Saving and Managing Your Money

As we said at the beginning, you only need a few tools to be successful in your plan. Two of those tools are a *checking account* and a *savings account*. We will discuss both of these in detail in this chapter. There is a strong link between saving money and personal autonomy. The basic purposes of this chapter are to illustrate that link, and to stress the importance of regular payments into savings.

Autonomy

Autonomy—psychological, emotional, and financial—should be the goal of every parent for every child. We want our children to become free of the psychological obstacles that might deter them; we want them to experience emotion without becoming victims to it; and we want them eventually to possess enough money to free them from a way of life that has come to be known as "strapped." Reaching some degree of this autonomy is a barometer by which a healthy adulthood is measured—at least for half the population. Unfortunately, for the half of the population that is the concern of this book, adulthood has always been measured by a very different barometer.

Autonomy is the art of self-governing, the art of reviewing our options and making those choices that will serve us best. The general tendency has been to teach women that their best option is to rely on others. As a result, their autonomy has been historically eroded and at times obliterated altogether. This is where the myth that "good girls are taken care of" overshadows the reality. This myth, which fosters the misconception that women are not served by being autonomous, has been hawked from political platform and pulpit alike, and parents have, more often than not, followed suit. It is not big news that parents have raised sons to leave their mark on the world and daughters to marry.

In lieu of autonomy, girls have been judged women on the basis of their ability to serve, to fit into the landscape, to bear and raise children, and to feel fulfilled by these functions. Now, our society has added holding down a full-time job to all of these other responsibilities. Women have all of the burdens and responsibilities of adulthood without the privileges of autonomy and choice.

Although we like to believe that women are more autonomous now than in the past, it is still true that many women keep their own checking accounts *until* they marry; but once they marry, their husbands handle the joint checking account, and they have very little or no control over the income of the house, even those portions of income to which their paychecks contribute.

There is nothing that will make you feel more childlike than to have to ask for money whenever you want to do something. There is nothing that will make you feel less empowered than never having your own funds.

So don't give up your financial autonomy. There is nothing wrong with a joint checking account so long as it is used for joint expenses. But when the joint account is used for all expenses, joint and individual, we have not seen one situation where there have not been hard feelings on both sides. It isn't fair to either party. Financially, you must make your own personal decisions.

One of our clients had been married for eighteen years and employed at the same company for nine of those years. Our client and her husband had roughly the same income. She came to see us under the guise of having a financial problem, but after we heard the story, we realized that the difficulty had very little to do with money. It turned out that there was a particular, modestly-priced car that she wanted to buy. Their incomes could well have afforded the car. In fact, her income alone could easily have afforded the car. She asked us repeatedly if she could afford the car and repeatedly we told her that financially, there was no question that she could buy the car.

Finally, the truth came out. Her husband had forbidden her to buy the car, even with her own money. After eighteen years of this relationship, she felt as though she had all the responsibilities of being an adult but few of the privileges.

In the technical sense, this was not a money problem. Financially, there was plenty of money to make the desired purchase. This was a very emotional problem, which had a money issue as its symptom.

We advised her to set up her own checking account and to urge her husband to do the same. We also advised her to keep the joint account, into which she and her husband could contribute equally, and to use the money in the joint account solely for joint expenses, such as the mortgage and utility bills. They could spend the money remaining in the individual accounts according to their individual wishes. And if she wanted to buy a car with her money, she should.

We ran into this client about a year later. She confessed that getting her own checking account had totally changed her life. She had begun to feel the power of handling her own money, of making her own decisions, and of creating her own choices. She felt healthier and happier than she had in years and admitted that, ironically, she had decided not to buy the car she wanted. When we looked surprised, she replied, "You don't understand. Once I had control of my own money, I realized that the argument about the car had really been about my lack of control. I just can't tell you how much healthier I feel these days."

Checking Accounts

In this section, we will answer questions such as, what is it?, and who needs it? You will learn about its cost-effectiveness, its usefulness for record keeping, and the reasons for balancing checking accounts. Finally, we will discuss choosing the right type of checking account.

What is a Checking Account?

A checking account is a service that most banks provide for their customers. A typical checking account works as follows: you deposit funds, and then you write checks to distribute those funds you have just deposited. Most people do not use checking accounts as vehicles to save money. Checking accounts are conveniences. They are a fast and efficient (but not necessarily easy) method that you can use to pay your bills. You receive a book of checks and a check register (to keep track of the checks you write), which allows you the convenience of not carrying cash. A person with a checking account simply writes checks for purchases or expenses based on the money that is in the account at the time the check is written.

Who Should Have a Checking Account?

Most people find checking accounts enormously convenient and much more cost-effective than money orders or cashier's checks, which can be very expensive. Checking accounts eliminate the hazards of carrying cash (loss or theft), and provide a permanent record of your transactions, because all checks are returned to you after they are cashed. However, checking accounts do require some record keeping (see section on record keeping below), which many people find inconvenient.

Checking accounts are an efficient way to pay monthly fixed expenses and controllable expenses, to obtain cash, and to cover any other expenses that might arise.

Who Should Not Have One. Anyone who writes checks for an amount greater than the funds in their account ("insufficient checks") will find their checking account will cost them more money than it will save them. It is not good business to write insufficient checks, and it's not taking good care of yourself. One client never opened her bank statements, never recorded a check in the check register, and, as you might imagine, was constantly writing insufficient checks.

These bounced checks cost a tremendous amount of money. First of all, consider the amount of the check itself, which must still be paid. Then consider the charge the bank will assess, which may range from $10 to $25 or higher, depending on the bank, and then consider the charge that is assessed by the company to whom the insufficient check was written. Suppose she bought something in a store for $15. If the check was insufficient, the store might charge her a returned check handling fee of $15, and the bank might charge her an NSF (non-sufficient funds) charge of $15;

so, that $15 purchase just cost $45, and it can all be attributed to poor record keeping. As we said before, this is not taking very good care of yourself.

If you currently have a checking account but are not using it to your advantange, take a good look at the problem. Don't harm yourself financially if you can avoid it. Congratulate yourself on this realization and take this opportunity to make a choice better suited to you. In the case of our particular client, she chose not to improve her record keeping, but rather to transact all her business with cash. She didn't mind the extra inconvenience. Cash suited her very well, and saved her a great deal of money.

How Are the Records of Checking Accounts Kept?

Each time you write a check, record in the check register the check number, the amount of the check, and the party to whom the check was issued. Always subtract the amount of the check from the checking account balance so you will know exactly how much money remains in the account.

If you have a cash card and use ATM (automatic teller machine) withdrawals, always record the amount of the cash withdrawal at the time you make it.

Once a month, the bank sends all checking account customers all the checks they've written that month. These are called "cancelled checks." Along with these cancelled checks will be an accounting statement showing all the transactions on the checking account during that same period of time. This statement will reflect the checks written, the money deposited into the checking account, any transfers of money made out of the account, any insufficient check charges, charges for services, a monthly service charge, a transfer fee, or any fee assessed for not complying with the requirements of the particular account.

How Do I Balance a Checking Account?

This is not a stupid question, and those of you who don't know how to perform this calculation are not alone. Of all the clients we counseled, only one client ever said that she balanced her checking account each and every month in accordance with the checking account bank statement that she received. Everyone else either didn't open the statement when it arrived, or opened it but didn't balance it.

There is only one valid reason to balance your statement: it proves that you have as much money in the account as you think you have! Otherwise, it is an intellectual activity that does not carry with it any moral consequences. You may get the impression that people who balance their checking accounts are good people and people who don't balance their checking accounts are bad people. This is a myth perpetrated by people who balance their checking accounts, and is emphatically not true!

We will say, however, that there is a very important reason for determining, on a monthly basis, that you and the bank agree. It is part of good record keeping, it is part of retaining control over your money, and it is critical if you intend to make sure that the bank is computing your account correctly.

Not balancing your checking account is a little like buying something at a store and never counting the change the cashier returns to you. Most people who hand a $20 bill over the counter for something that costs $6.72 will count the change. Oddly, those same people will deposit hundreds of dollars each month in their checking account, write checks for hundreds of dollars, and never look at a bank statement.

The fundamentals of balancing a typical checking account are spelled out on the back of the checking account bank statement. It is a step-by-step process. However, if you have trouble following the instructions, just take your checkbook, your bank statement, and your cancelled checks into the bank and ask a bank employee to show you how to balance it. If you have a good friend who knows how to do it, ask them. Don't feel embarrassed. We can assure you, you are in the majority.

Choosing the Right Type of Checking Account

Depending on which financial institution you're dealing with, you may be offered a variety of types of checking accounts. However, they can basically be divided into two categories: (1) those that earn interest, and (2) those that do not.

Banks may offer many deals when it comes to checking accounts. These may include: accounts that bear interest; accounts that do not bear interest; accounts that require a minimum balance to be kept in them at all times; accounts that charge a monthly service charge; accounts that allow you to overdraft; and accounts that can be connected to other accounts you have at the bank. The list is quite long and will vary from bank to bank. Any bank employee should be able to explain all the options to you. They usually are willing to do this because they are anxious to get and keep your business.

Your choice here is quite simple. You will want to put your money in an interest-bearing account if your institution offers one. It may mean maintaining a minimum balance in the checking account or in a savings account, or some other requirement. Whatever the requirement is, if you can meet it without financial harm to yourself, it is always in your best interest to keep your money in just such an account and allow the bank to pay you interest.

Besides minimum balance requirements, be aware of the other requirements on an account that you choose. Some accounts allow the holder to write only a certain number of checks per month without incurring a service charge. Other accounts charge a set fee every month, regardless of the number of checks written. Still others charge you by the check.

For example, one of our clients had a checking account that assessed a service charge if more than ten checks were written per month. She consistently wrote more than ten checks per month, so her account was consistently charged the service charge. Naturally, we advised her to change the type of checking account she was using, because that account was actually costing her money, where another type of account might save her money.

Conclusion

A checking account can be the least expensive way to manage your money and keep good records. Opening your own checking account, and managing it well, are small steps that can generate great results.

Savings

In this section we will examine the reasons for saving and how your purposes can best be served by a combination of working savings, special savings, and reserve savings. Developing the best savings plan will involve considering various banking options. We provide some basic information concerning interest. Then we describe the basic types of accounts and institutions. Finally, we will discuss diversification as an important part of your overall savings plan.

Now that you have a handle on your income, fixed expenses and controllable expenses, and a relatively good idea of how your plan is shaping up, it's time to look at the role savings will play in your plan.

Why Save Money?

We all know it's a good idea to save money; our mothers and grandmothers told us so. But why, especially when we need money *now?* The *practical* reason is that money saved may protect you against adverse events and give you more choices in almost every area of your life. The *emotional* reason is that planning ahead and taking good care of yourself by saving is an expression of that uniquely adult prerogative, autonomy.

We have heard many times that millions of Americans are only one paycheck away from homelessness. Many of our clients were in this position when they came to us. We have watched them, in amazingly short periods of time, use a balanced plan to increase their savings. Was this a good thing? Yes!

One client lost her job and had the luxury of living on her savings for several extra months while looking for the job that suited her best. Others have had the satisfaction of taking fully-paid vacations, doing expensive house repairs, or starting new businesses.

These examples illustrate the practical reasons for saving. But we feel a more important reason, especially for women, is that having financial resources enhances a person's autonomy.

What does autonomy have to do with saving money?

Saving money is one of the kindest, most respectful things you can do for yourself. It is a critical contribution to your autonomy and process of self-empowerment. We place a great deal of emphasis on saving regularly because we have witnessed the benefits first hand. As we have watched our clients build their savings accounts through regular contributions, we have also watched the corresponding growth of their personal power and self-esteem. They realized that paying themselves not only increased their financial security, but also repeatedly sent a clear message of care and concern for someone they had overlooked for too long—themselves.

Set aside the myths that interfere with your autonomy. Measure your adulthood by a realistic standard. Without a regularly-funded savings account, your financial security may be tenuous and your ability to choose may be threatened. Creating our own choices, having those choices available, and exercising our powers to choose, transform us from adults who see only burdens and responsibilities, to adults who see the possibilities in life.

What If You Have Debts—Shouldn't You Pay Those First, Before Saving Any Money?

Absolutely not. Remember that the primary rule of your financial plan is balance. It is possible, and necessary, to save money even if you have substantial debts. Your goal is to be as aggressive about building your assets as you are about decreasing your liabilities. For an example, see the section on page 107 entitled, "How Much Money Should You Deposit Into Working Savings?"

There are three types of savings in our program: *working savings, special savings,* and *reserve savings.* We will discuss them each in turn.

Working Savings

What is Working Savings?

Your working savings is a bank account into which you deposit money every time you get paid. It is not an untouchable account. In fact, one of its two purposes is to provide a pool of cash that you can use when expenses arise which do not fall into your categories of fixed and controllable expenses. The other purpose is to provide money for your reserve savings. All this will be explained more fully below.

Deposit Money Into Working Savings Every Paycheck

Funding this working savings account will be a primary part of your plan. The amount you decide to deposit into this savings account will be consistent and deposited, without fail, every payday. This amount will become part of your list of fixed expenses, and payment of this amount into that account will be like the payment of other bills.

Let's look again at our example from the previous chapters.

Monthly income		$1600
Less fixed expenses		
Rent	$425	
Electric	60	
Gas	40	
Water	18	
Phone	35	
Cable	20	
Insurance	90	
Loans	275	
Newspaper	5	
Subtotal		- 968
Money left		$ 632
Less savings		- 25
Subtotal		$ 607
Less controllables		
Food	$250	
House mnt.	15	
Transp.	45	
Entertnmnt.	60	
Credit cards	35	
Charge cards	0	
Charity	18	
Addictions	30	
Clothing	30	
Beauty shop	20	
Subtotal		- 253
Money left		$ 104

Please note that the payment to savings is made *before* you begin to pay those expenses that are controlled by you. If you are paid twice a month, you may end up dividing in half the $25 you have decided to pay, so that you pay $12.50 from each paycheck. Of course, keep in mind that after you make your plan for each paycheck, depending on the time constraints of some of your other bills, you could decide to pay the whole $25 out of only one check.

How Much Money Should You Deposit Into Working Savings?

This depends on your personal financial situation, but two rules apply: First, some money, no matter how little, should be deposited every paycheck. One client started her savings plan by paying five dollars a month. It sounds ridiculous, doesn't it? But only eighteen months later, she had savings of more than $2,500. We will explain how she did this later. Second, the amount that is deposited should be in balance with your overall financial situation. You would like to get to the point where you are paying at least as much toward building your assets as toward decreasing your liabilities. Eventually, you would like to tip the scales in your favor by continually building your assets while taking on debt at a moderate rate under your control.

If you are like most of our clients, you have some obvious debts and very few assets. The main goal of this money-management plan is to always decrease your liabilities while increasing your assets. Assets are all the things you own and liabilities are all the things you owe. If you rent, you don't own your residence; if you own a house, chances are the bank owns most of it. You may own your car outright, but if you do not, the bank or finance company will own most of that too. Your most obvious asset is money—this includes money you have on hand, in the bank, in a checking account, a savings account, or a certificate of deposit (CD). The *only* way to build this asset is to *save*. There is absolutely no other alternative.

Let's look at our example once more. Our hypothetical client pays $275 to loans, $35 to credit cards, and $0 to charge cards. That's a total of $310 per month toward decreasing her liabilities. She'd like to eventually get to the point where at least that much is being paid toward building her assets, but at this point, that would obviously be impossible. So, she examines the amount of money she has left after she's paid her controllables and finds $129. If she attempted to put the entire $129 into working savings every month, she would be caught all month without money to fall back on. This would be a decision made without much sense of balance and without much regard for herself. So, after considering the possible needs for the money each month, she decides that paying $25 each month to her savings will not be a hardship or leave her without funds, and will be an excellent first step toward building working savings, which are going to be so helpful to her down the line.

Once she has decided on $25, paying that amount to savings each month becomes as imperative in her mind as paying the $425 to rent. By paying her rent and utilities, she makes sure that she has a place to live, and by paying her savings account, she makes sure that she has assets. She is on her way to becoming financially autonomous.

How Much Money Should You Keep in a Working Savings Account?

Again, the answer to this is very personal and very simple. It truly depends on the individual and what the individual wants to accomplish with that particular asset. And there is one more important factor that we call the *level of comfortability*. If you feel comfortable with a particular number, it is the right number for you. If you just want a rule of thumb, we feel that two months' take-home pay is a suitable goal for a single person. However, realize that this is a personal decision that should be made with awareness.

We counseled one young man who was married with one child. He determined, after much thought, that his level of comfortability was $1,200. When we asked him how he arrived at that, he said his house payment was $400 per month and he felt comfortable with at least three house payments in a savings account. When we asked him why three, why not four or two, he answered that he just felt deep inside that if he were to lose his job, it would never take him more than three months to find another. With three house payments in working savings, he would know that he and his family would be assured of a place to live.

We cautioned him about considering other expenses for that three-month period which would naturally arise (food, utilities, other fixed and controllable expenses, or the unexpected needs of his daughter). These were things he had not considered. He chose to revamp his figure to $2,100. We cannot say exactly why he picked $2,100 instead of $2,000 or $2,500, but he felt much better about it.

We counseled a woman who had spent five years working on our plan attempting to recover from debt she had been burdened with after she got divorced. After having worked so hard to become debt-free, her level of comfortability was much higher than our young man's. She insisted that she could not feel secure without at least $10,000 in working savings at any one time, and once she made that a priority in her life, she funded that account until it reached the $10,000 mark. Because she was a single woman, living very modestly, we suggested that $10,000 might be a bit high for her particular circumstances, and that she might move part of that into reserve savings to be invested. However (and this is where the psychological and emotional qualities begin to factor in), she had felt so terribly strapped after her divorce that she was convinced she never wanted to go through that again. She wanted plenty of available money for anything she hadn't anticipated. The truth was, it just helped her sleep better at night knowing that she had provided for herself to the extent of $10,000 in working savings.

There are many factors to consider when making your decision. Women with children will want to consider factors that women alone do not need to examine. Women with partners who are dependable financially may not need as much in working savings as women with partners who are financially irresponsible. This is a good time to examine your emotions, though. Quite often, our clients picked a figure based solely on emotional factors. It is wise to use a combination of the two. Review the practical considerations and give credence to the emotional elements as well. Balance is the key, and in balance you will find your deepest power.

Increase the Amount You Deposit as You Are Able

Remember the client who started off saving $5 a paycheck and had saved $2,500 in only eighteen months? There were two ways she did this. Under her plan, she steadily chipped away at her debts. As each one was paid off, she paid the money she had used monthly to pay that debt into working savings instead. By the time she reached the $2,500 mark, she was allocating $175 per month to working savings.

You will be very surprised how quickly these balances rise, even if you can only begin by paying $5 per month into a new working savings account. As your debts are eliminated, more of your monthly money is freed, and if you wisely reallocate that money into the job of building your assets, you will never regret it.

The second way she rapidly increased her savings was by her wise use of acceleration income. As you will recall from our income chapter, acceleration money is income that you do not receive on a regular monthly basis and that allows you to accelerate your plan. For example, if you received a refund of $2,000 on your income taxes, this refund would be considered acceleration money. In the process of deciding exactly what to do with the money, you would want to look at several factors such as:

- How much money do I have in my working savings account?
- Have I reached my level of comfortability?
- Should I change my level of comfortability?
- What is my debt situation? Do my debts still outweigh my assets by a great amount?

All of these questions should be addressed, but let's give you another example that might make the process clear.

Let's return to our hypothetical client who has the monthly income of $1,600. Let's say further that she has been on the plan for several months and has managed to develop her working savings to a balance of $1,800 and her comfortability goal was $2,100. Let's say also that she has been diligently chipping away at her debts, but she has these outstanding bills left:

Visa	$ 472	18%
MasterCard	250	15%
Sears	700	10%
Student loan	2200	5%
Total	$3622	

So, this is the scenario. She has just received a check from the IRS for $2,000 as a refund on taxes. Many of our real-life clients spent the refund faster than it took the ink to dry on the check. Many of them put the entire $2,000 toward the debt, paying off $2,000 of the total $3,622, leaving them with debts of $1,622 remaining and no increase in their assets. This is not a good allocation of that $2,000. Please don't overlook the importance of balance. We cannot stress enough the desire to create balance in every area of your life, beginning with finances.

With balance in mind, let's look at a better solution to our problem of what to do with the $2,000. First of all, let's put $300 of the $2,000 into the working savings to increase it from $1,800 to $2,100, thereby reaching the client's predetermined level of comfortability.

Let's also use $500 of the remaining $1,700 to establish the first deposit into the reserve savings. (See discussion below.)

The remaining $1,200 can be used to pay off debt and to treat yourself to something. For example, let's pay off the Visa and MC (which would leave us with $478 from the original $2,000) and then keep the $78 for ourselves to do with as we like. The remaining $400 can be used toward the Sears bill, an additional deposit toward the reserve savings, or for some extraordinary expense such as new tires for the car or a small house repair.

The important thing to remember is that building your assets is as important as decreasing your liabilities, and savings accounts must be funded, regularly and with acceleration money.

What Should You Use Your Working Savings For?

Client opinions on this ranged from one extreme to the other. Either clients felt they needed to save thousands of dollars and never touch it, or they felt free to save next to nothing and use what little there was for every possible contingency. In short, the clients wanted either to account for everything or to account for nothing. Again, we stress balance. Somewhere in the middle is the realistic approach to your working savings.

We call it working savings because it will work for you. You will fund it with scrupulous regularity, and in return, any bill that arises that is not a fixed expense or a controllable expense will be paid out of the working savings.

For example, if you pay a personal property tax bill and the bill can be paid in one lump sum annually, in two six-month installments, or in four quarterly payments, but cannot be paid monthly, it would be impractical for you to try to list it as either a fixed or a controllable expense. You should pay the property tax bill in four quarterly payments from the money available to you in your working savings.

Another example would be that month when everyone you know has a birthday. Most of us go for months without ever having to buy a simple birthday gift. Then, a month will roll around when no less than five of our closest relatives and friends have chosen to have their birthdays. In many cases, if only one birthday comes up, you can take care of the gift with the money you have left after paying fixed and controllable expenses. But it would be difficult for anyone to absorb five birthdays in one month, so you will want to dip into working savings.

When you spend money out of working savings, don't feel guilty. There is no need to worry. You are in control. Unexpected bills or unanticipated needs for money are precisely the reasons you fund your working savings. You cannot hold yourself responsible for knowing *every single need for money that can possibly arise*. But you can prepare yourself for what you cannot anticipate.

Special Savings

Don't use your working savings for large amounts such as a down payment on a house or a new car. Instead, feel free to open a special savings account to save up for a vacation, a new car, a down payment on a house, or any other special, expensive item. If you save $5,000 as a down payment on a house in a special account for that purpose, when it comes time to buy the house, feel free to use that entire $5,000. You are not jeopardizing your security by draining a special account of all the money for which it was intended.

Reserve Savings

Part of life is uncertainty. As we tried to emphasize in the introduction, no one can have absolute control of absolutely everything. By funding and making use of a working savings account, you send messages of confidence to yourself—confidence in your ability to handle unexpected needs, should they arise. By successfully building the working savings to your particular level of comfortability, you have taken a giant first step toward autonomy, toward independent decision-making, and toward personal empowerment.

At times, however, your need for money may far exceed the amount available to you in your working savings. You might unexpectedly lose your job, you may have an unplanned child and need a bigger residence, or a loved one who has contributed to the household might die. There are many more situations that can arise without warning, which can be demanding or even devastating financially if you have not provided well for yourself. For these occasions you will want and need a reserve savings.

How Does Reserve Savings Differ From Working Savings?

A reserve savings is one that you hope you will not need to touch. This is money that, as they used to say in the old days, is "put away for a rainy day." And of course, we all hope that that rainy day never comes. It is truly *emergency* money, meant only to be used in an emergency of such proportion that you cannot handle the problem within the framework of fixed expenses, controllable expenses, or working savings. It is your third line of financial defense. If you are presently living with basically no checking account, no working savings, and no reserve savings, you are virtually defenseless when and if a financial problem should arise. Your first line of defense is to establish your plan with regard to fixed and controllable expenses, and establish a checking account. Your second line of financial defense is to fund and use a working savings account in order to accommodate those needs outside of your fixed or controllable expenses. And your third line of defense is to fund and have a reserve savings in the event of an emergency that your other lines of defense cannot absorb.

How Do I Fund a Reserve Savings?

The answer to this will be quite pleasing to you. Your main goal is to decrease your liabilities while building your assets. In building your assets, the first step is to start and fund regularly the working savings. When your working savings has reached your pre-determined level of comfortability, you do not stop making savings payments. You simply continue to pay the working savings account regularly as usual, and transfer any excess money into what will now be called your reserve savings. By excess, we mean, any money in the working savings that exceeds the balance you had decided to carry in that account. The reserve savings is actually a separate bank account.

To show how the reserve savings works, let's return to our hypothetical client. Her comfortability level was $2,100. Any time her working savings went above that amount, she tranferred the excess funds to her reserve savings account. When unexpected car repairs arose in the amount of $600, she confidently withdrew $600 from working savings, knowing that her regular payments to savings would restore that account to her comfortability level of $2,100. Her reserve savings stayed at the same level until her working savings was replenished, at which time the reserve savings started increasing once more.

Banking Options

With all this talk about savings accounts, it might be helpful to know a few facts about banking and banking institutions: banks, savings and loans (also called "thrifts"), and credit unions.

Even though there are technical differences between these institutions, and the institutions themselves are careful about preserving the distinctions, for the sake of convenience, we are referring to them all as "banks." If we do make a point that is particular to one type of institution, we will specify which type, to avoid confusion.

About Interest

We're going to make this very easy for you. If you deposit money in a bank, you are known as a "depositor," and the bank will *pay* you interest for the privilege of keeping your money. If you borrow money from a bank, you are known as the "borrower," and the institution will *charge* you interest for the privilege of borrowing money. These are the ways in which banks keep customers and make money.

Banks have many ways to make money; the primary way is by lending money ("making loans") at a particular interest rate. The interest paid to the bank when the borrower repays the loan is income for the bank. Banks will not stay in business for very long if they lend money at a lesser percentage of interest than the percentage they pay out to depositors.

In other words, banks cannot pay 15 percent interest on the money you deposit in their bank if they lend money to borrowers at only 6 percent. They would be in the same situation as any individual who earns $1,000 in salary but consistently has monthly expenses of $2,000. Eventually, the imbalance will catch up with both the person and the bank, and they will become insolvent.

The percentage of interest that will be paid to you is based on several factors, but largely on what that particular bank can charge for lending money. If it can make loans at only 9 percent, it will probably not pay its depositors 7 percent on their money. It needs to make enough income to make a profit.

Usually, the spread is more like this. A loan is paid back at 13 percent, while a savings account accrues interest at 6 percent.

There are many other types of accounts, which may be called by different names and vary from bank to bank, but the basic premise is always the same. You deposit your money into the account at the bank, and the bank pays you a certain amount of interest for leaving it there.

The second rule to remember about all savings instruments is that the longer the bank keeps your money, the more money it is willing to pay you for the privilege. In other words, the regular savings, where you can withdraw any portion of your money at any time may pay only 6 percent, but a certificate of deposit (CD) that requires you to leave your money in the bank for a certain period of time (1 year), may pay you 7 percent in interest.

Compound Interest

Compound interest means making interest on your interest. For example, you deposit $100 into a savings account at 6 percent interest. In one year, the bank has paid you $6 in interest. If you leave the money in the bank, the next year you are beginning to make what is known as "compound interest." This means that for the second year, the 6 percent interest that the bank is paying you will be paid on the balance of $106, not on the original $100 that you deposited. Because of this, your interest the second year will be $6.36 rather than $6.00.

These are small sums for the sake of an example. But the beauty of compound interest is well known to real savers. Let's take an example using numbers that may be more realistic for you.

Let's say you can afford to save $5 per month and that's all you will ever be able to save (highly unlikely). If you consistently put $5 per month into your savings account, and your savings account paid you an average of 6 percent annually on your balance, after ten years your balance would be $816. After twenty years it would be $2,278. After thirty years it would be $4,896. This may or may not seem like a lot to you at first glance, but consider this. In thirty years, if you're only depositing $5 per month, you've only deposited a total of $1,800 of your own money, and yet your account balance is $4,896. The difference of $3,096 is interest paid to you by the institution.

Consider also that it is highly unlikely that over the course of your life you will only be able to consistently afford $5 per month. The truth is your contributions to savings will become much greater than they are when you start the plan, and increasing your deposits will only make the interest you earn on your money that much greater.

Pick up a book from the library on compound interest. It will have lots of facts that you will find hard to believe, but the numbers don't lie. For example, if you somehow received a windfall of $5,000, and deposited the full amount in an account paying 6 percent interest, that $5,000 would turn into $10,000 in twelve years. If you could deposit that same $5,000 into an account paying 9 percent interest, it would become $10,000 in only eight years, and if it were deposited in an account paying 12 percent interest, it would grow to $10,000 in only six years.

Is There a Rule of Thumb about Bank Accounts?

Yes! There is one thing you can count on. The more money you have in any given institution, the better the deal you will get on your checking and savings accounts. For example, one of our clients had a $2,500 CD and a regular checking account. We examined her checking account statement to find that a $5 service charge was assessed on the account each month. We suggested that she speak to the teller on her next visit, because in many cases, the bank will connect various accounts in the same bank and by doing this, eliminate the service charges. This was the case at her bank, and the $5 charge was omitted from then on. This was a savings to her of $60 per year.

Types of Accounts

Banks offer a variety of savings instruments such as:

- regular savings
- passbook savings
- money market accounts
- certificates of deposit

To briefly describe each of the above, let's put this as simply as possible. All four of these instruments involve you depositing money into an account at the bank.

Regular Savings. The regular savings is "totally liquid," meaning you can withdraw or deposit money at any time.

Passbook savings. The passbook savings is the same as a regular savings except for the fact that you are given a passbook that the bank teller will up-date each time you make a deposit or withdrawal. (This is often a very handy motivator when you are trying to build a savings account because you can always look at your passbook and know exactly what your balance is. Also, you can see, at a glance, how much progress you have made.)

Money Market Accounts. The money market accounts usually pay a slightly higher rate of interest because they have certain restrictions about depositing or withdrawing money. You may be able to deposit as often as you like, but be able to withdraw only a certain number of times per month without a penalty. There may also be a minimum balance (for example, $2,000) required on such an account. Keep in mind that banks are willing to pay higher rates of interest for the privilege of restricting, even minimally, your access to your own funds.

Certificates of Deposit. Lastly, the certificates of deposit (commonly know as CDs) are the most restrictive of the four. A CD is an account in which you deposit a lump sum of money, for example $3,500, and sign a contract with the bank to leave it in the account for a particular length of time, such as six months, one year, eighteen months, two years. If you should need to withdraw your $3,500 before the time period has expired, you may do so but you probably will have to pay a penalty for the privilege. You should find out all about the early withdrawal penalty before purchasing a CD.

Where to Keep Your Working Savings

You should keep your working savings in a savings account (passbook or regular) or a money market account. Because, by definition, the working savings is an account from which you may frequently draw, you will obviously not want that money in an account that places any restrictions on how much or how often you may withdraw your funds.

Where to Keep Your Reserve Savings

Because your intention would be not to have to touch the balance in the reserve savings, you might want to place that money in a more restrictive account, which pays a higher rate of interest.

Choosing a Financial Institution

Banks, savings and loans ("thrifts") and credit unions all offer consumer services, such as checking accounts, savings accounts, and consumer loans. Visit several institutions, and compare their services, their interest rates on accounts, and their charges (if any) for their services.

Banks and Savings and Loans. The consumer services offered by banks and savings and loans are now essentially the same.

Credit Unions. Credit unions are usually formed for a particular group of people who are called "members." For example: A company may provide a credit union for its employees; State workers may have their own credit union; There may be a teachers' credit union or a credit union specifically for the employees of a particular hospital. When you deposit money into a savings account in a credit union, you become a member, and depending on your balance, you are the owner of a certain number of credit union shares.

There are many rules that govern how you deposit or withdraw money from a credit union, none of which are particularly complicated or restrictive. The main thing to remember about credit unions is this: credit unions will often pay higher rates of interest on depository accounts because they have fewer loans go bad.

Here's how this works. A loan "goes bad" when the borrower has "defaulted," which means borrowed money and not paid it back. Because credit unions serve a certain group, one of their basic rules is that any loans are paid back through "payroll deduction." This means that, essentially, so long as you keep working, they will get their money even before you get your paycheck. Consequently, they tend to have fewer bad debts and can afford to lend money more often than a bank or savings and loan, which have to rely on borrowers to mail in their payment checks. Credit unions can also afford to pay slightly higher interest rates on deposits.

Some credit union accounts require savings depositers to maintain a minimum balance in order to borrow a certain amount of money. In short, they keep you honest and keep your debt from getting too large for your assets.

Regardless of which type of financial institution you decide on, investigate, don't be shy. Walk right in and sit down with a customer service representative and ask them all about the savings accounts their institution offers. If you are not treated with courtesy and respect, or if you get the impression that the institution does not care whether it has your financial business, march right out and visit another bank, savings and loan, or credit union. There are plenty of institutions that treat their customers well and have loyal customers for many years as proof. Don't do business with a financial institution that doesn't make you feel powerful.

With financial institutions, bigger is not necessary better. Many of our clients reported feeling much more comfortable with a smaller institution, because they felt the employees of the institution knew them, cared about them, and took an active interest in their financial success.

When Should You Think About "Investments?"

A deposit in a savings account is an "investment." However, your financial condition will eventually reach the point where more diverse investing becomes a realistic option. You will know when you have reached this point. A good rule of thumb is to ask yourself the following questions:

- Are my fixed and controllable expenses all in line with my income?
- Have I funded my working savings to my level of comfortability?
- Have I funded my reserve savings to an appropriate level? (Because all your savings past the working savings are reserve savings, the appropriate level becomes a question of personal preference. When do *you* feel comfortable moving your money from a very safe account to something a little riskier?)
- Do I have an amount of debt that is not burdensome?

If the answers to these four questions are yes, then you are probably ready to begin thinking about such things as stocks, bonds, and mutual funds. These instruments are not within the scope of this book, and we want to reiterate that investing in these vehicles is inappropriate if you cannot answer yes, with a smile on your face, to the above four questions.

Let us make one other comment. Many people feel safer with their money in a bank, even if the balance is thousands of dollars and they are debt-free. Many people do not sleep well at night if their money is in what they consider to be "risky" ventures, even if those ventures are very reputable stocks.

Here's where the psychological and emotional factors come into play. Give that side of you the attention it deserves. If you can make 8 percent in a CD and a 10 percent return in a mutual fund, but the mutual fund will make you such a nervous wreck that you'll eat up the 2 percent in therapy trying to calm down, or the 2 percent will be absorbed when you have to pay a commission to the broker that got you into the mutual fund, don't cave in to social pressure. Don't be greedy. Be good to yourself. Saving money will never hurt you. Sure, you might make slightly more in a slightly more risky instrument, but you might live a happier, mentally healthier life by doing what you really feel is safe. Make a good decision based on your needs and desires, and don't let anyone talk you out of it.

Diversify

You've probably seen old bankers in the movies with cigars hanging out of the sides of their mouths mumble "diversify." Better advice, oddly enough, has never been given.

Diversify means "not putting all your eggs in one basket." And contrary to the popular belief that only the rich have enough money to need to diversify, everyone should be aware of diversification at all times. Whether you have a bank account of $100,000, or an account of $1,000, if that's all the money you have in the world, losing it would cause you great financial concern. In fact, if you were the person with the $1,000 balance, losing all of it would probably mean bigger problems for you than the other person losing a hundred times that much.

It's always a good policy to divide your assets among different institutions. For instance, a savings account in one bank, a CD in another, an IRA in another. This is just playing it safe.

Conclusion

Do we need large bank accounts in order to feel good about ourselves? Of course not! Money, even if it's stockpiled in banks all over the world, will not, by itself, give us self-esteem and confidence. However, the activity of controlling your own money and choosing to fund an account for yourself shows you that you care about yourself, and that you have discipline, motivation, and confidence. These factors all contribute to higher self-esteem. And, we assure you, savings accounts will grow if you contribute to them regularly as part of your plan. And money in the bank to fall back on during difficult times will help you feel more secure and less vulnerable. Don't forget that the breathing room created by a solid savings account helps increase your options, which in itself, will contribute to your feelings of personal power.

Part of a complete lifetime financial plan is a devotion to retirement savings, discussed in the next chapter.

CHAPTER SEVEN

Retirement

I was sixteen that summer, working in a burned-out skeleton of a jewelry factory, unable to breathe because of the heat that moved and settled heavily by the grace of a few fans, and the acid stench rising from the plating vats only a few feet away.

The noon bell sounded and all of us rose immediately from our bench seats, heading for the nearest truck vendor for the lunch that we'd have to swallow whole in order to grab a few minutes from the precious thirty that was allowed us.

The old woman rose from the bench, by-passed the vendor trucks and made her feeble way to the one and only pay phone in the place. She waited in line for her turn, glancing at the black clock above the time cards, watching her liberty erode.

"Didn't you get any lunch?" I asked her when we were seated at our benches once again.

"No," she answered quietly.

"It must have been a very important phone call to keep you from eating?" I inquired further with the lack of grace that usually plagues sixteen-year-olds.

"Had to call the bill man," she replied.

"The bill man?"

"Yea, I've got lots of bills and if you don't call them and send them money, they take back your things. Some things you just can't afford to be without," she added.

"What about your husband?" I asked.

"Dead," she responded dryly.

"Why don't you retire?" I asked, with less sensitivity than I'd have imagined possible years later.

"Retire?" she inquired, her small blue eyes dull with fatigue. "This is retirement," she replied with a tiny sardonic smile.

Part of a solid money-management plan is saving for retirement. Retirement saving is distinct from the three lines of defense we mentioned in the previous chapter, but is an important part of an overall plan for financial autonomy.

In this chapter, we will define retirement, and then explain our belief that you may not be able to count on others to contribute to your retirement or rely on social security to provide a comfortable retirement. We will go on to analyze the ingredients of the most effective retirement plans and how you can go about making the most informed and beneficial choices for yourself. We will define IRA, SEP, and 401-K plans and tell you where to go for further advice.

What Is Retirement?

Retirement is the ability to stop working at a certain age without becoming financially devastated. Most Americans want to retire between the ages of 62 and 65, but more and more are attempting to retire early. The alternative to retiring is to continue working. It is that simple.

Retirement is not magic. It does not automatically happen. The ability to retire requires conscious planning throughout your life. And in this, as in all else that we've discussed in this book, the myth of "being taken care of" is unfortunately very, very strong.

Women's Retirement Myths

When a woman looks seriously at her intention to retire at some future date, many myths will arise. Some of the most common of these are expressed in the following comments:

- "Don't worry about it; your husband will handle it."
- "Don't be ridiculous, your parents have money, don't they?"
- "Don't worry, you've got good kids; they'll take care of you."
- "Doesn't your company have a great pension plan? Well then, you're all set."
- "Oh, the government will make sure there's social security. Really."
- "You're so young. Don't think about that now. Live your life, for heaven's sake!"
- "If you start planning for retirement, you're sure as hell going to die an early death."
- "You can find a better use for that money. After all, won't your oldest be needing a car next year?"

All of you have heard these comments and probably other similar suggestions on the lack of need for good retirement planning.

All of them are based on myths, fears, and denial, both social and personal, and should be discounted immediately!

It may, indeed, come to pass that you have a domestic partner who provides well for both of you in retirement, your parents manage to leave you a sizeable sum at the time of their deaths, your offspring make a zillion dollars and support you lavishly, your employer is a rock of Gibraltar when it comes to pension plans, or the government strikes gold on the moon and funds social security effortlessly. While one or all of these things might intervene to provide you with a blissful retirement, the opposite scenarios are being played out every day in every city of our nation with much greater frequency.

And the truth is women are far less likely to have retirement funds than men. That does not mean that women are incapable of consciously arranging their own retirement plans. It means that all women, even life-long, full-time working women, make far less money in their lifetimes than men, are bombarded from an early age with clear message myths telling them to take care of everyone else in their lives but themselves, and, in financial partnerships (such as a domestic partnership), tend to earn less and accrue less in retirement benefits than their partners.

Think of retirement as a cake. What you do for yourself is the cake, and what others do for you is the icing.

The Icing

The icing on your retirement cake is anything that others do for you. These others include your employers, government, partners, husbands, parents, and children. Let's look at each of these retirement sources.

Employers

Companies are unreliable. And while some companies are clearly better to their employees than other companies, no company is completely trustworthy.

Companies are organizations that can be bought and sold, have their boards of directors change, have their owners die, have family members inherit—the truth is, there are as many possible changes in companies as there are in human relationships. Even the most steadfast company can be bought by a bigger company for the sole purpose of depleting a substantial pension fund and then closing the company.

You may have legal recourse in such an event, but who wants to be in that position? After working for forty years and expecting to receive a large sum of money, or a monthly annuity, instead you're stuck with hiring a lawyer, starting litigation, and going after money that is probably gone in an attempt to retrieve only a percentage of what you originally thought you would have to live on.

Companies also fail, for a variety of reasons. It doesn't necessarily mean that someone has their hand in the till, or that there has been poor management. Companies can fail based on the economy, the death of the owner, product obsolescence, a change in the laws, a change in the cost of raw materials, a change in the need for a particular service—the list is long.

Government

Companies look positively stable next to governments—which should give you some idea of how you ought to feel about social security.

There has not been a presidential election in our lifetime that has not mentioned the social security fund, usually by referring to it as "teetering on the brink of non-existence." The government runs on a deficit that cannot be pronounced because of the number of zeros to the left of the decimal point.

We certainly all hope that there will be some measure of social security there for us when we reach an eligible age, but again, we want to point out that this will be the icing on the cake; the cake you're going to have to bake yourself.

Partners/Husbands

Does it matter if you're in a domestic partnership? Our answer is "No," without reservation. The single woman who becomes aware of her personal need for a retirement plan is no different from a woman in a domestic partnership. In terms of planning strategy, it is the same: *All women must have their own retirement plans.*

Once you make up your mind to plan for your retirement, you will begin to fund a plan. If you are single, the plan must be set up to afford you the maximum amount of benefit. If you are in a domestic partnership, that plan may be funded by you, your partner, or by both of you, equally or unequally; but what is critical is that the plan must be set up to be of equal benefit to both partners.

It is common to see marriages where the husband, both through company plans and through personal plans, has generously funded his retirement years, while his wife has *no* retirement plans at all. The assumption usually is that: (1) He has her listed as the beneficiary on all the plans in the event of his death; and (2) They will remain partners throughout their lives.

STOP! STOP! STOP!

Ask yourself these questions if you are currently in this kind of arrangement or if you're thinking of entering into one:

- Do I really want to be asking my husband for money *all* of my life, until the day I die?
- Can I guarantee that our partnership will last for the rest of our lives?

- Do I really want to inherit a large sum of money in my elderly years if I have had no knowledge of how to handle it during the course of my life?
- If the partnership does not last, do I really want to be in the position of fighting for a fair share as part of a legal suit or for my rightful share because it was arranged that way up front?

We had a client who was forty-five years old, with two children, whose husband had been a long-time employee of a local utility company with an excellent pension plan.

They had gotten divorced about two years before we saw her. She had $200 in a savings account, a checking account with a minimal balance, no retirement funds whatsoever, two dependents, and a job that paid her about $42,000 a year.

At first glance, you might say, "great salary." But, look closer. The pension plan, generously funded by her husband and his company during the years of their marriage, had been completely lost to her during the divorce. While her own company paid a good salary, she had only recently acquired the job, and its pension plan did not even come close to the plan at her ex-husband's company. We're sure many of you will agree that $42,000 does not go too terribly far with two growing children, even though there was additional child support from their father. And perhaps most crucial of all was the glaringly obvious fact that she had approximately twenty-three years left to fund her retirement.

This is not to imply that one cannot fund a retirement in twenty-three years. The point is this: Compare a retirement fund based on twenty-three years of savings to one based on forty-three years. Her husband had begun working for the utility company when he was twenty-two.

If you're a full-time employee with a clear sense of what you're doing with your money, and you're in a domestic partnership, there is nothing stopping you from handling your own retirement plans and funding them solely on your own. Your partner is free to do the same.

However, if you're in a domestic partnership, and you and your partner agreed to handle retirement in some mutually beneficial way, then it must be done with equity and awareness.

A good domestic partnership is invaluable. If you and your partner see eye to eye on most things, particularly money, the likelihood of your planning and executing a retirement arrangement that agrees with both of you is very good. The likelihood that your partnership will successfully squirrel away money for later years is very high, and the chances are good that you will both be satisfied with your decisions if they are mutually made and if you both feel as though you're pulling in the same direction.

But domestic partnerships can work against you just as easily. It wasn't that long ago that married partners could assign beneficiary rights to someone other than their partner without having to let the partner know. The result was, of course, that many wives watched hundreds of thousands of dollars in employee pension funds go to someone other than themselves at the time of their husband's death. Companies now will require approval by the spouse if a partner is listing someone other than the spouse as a beneficiary.

Parents and Children

Unless your name is Dupont or Vanderbilt, don't assume the money your parents have will come to you. The number of factors that can intervene between parents and children is limitless. Let's name a few:

- Your parents sustain large medical bills in their old age, which completely deplete their entire savings.
- Your parents get totally overtaken with the idea of joining the Peace Corps, give up all their worldly

possessions, don a knapsack and hiking shoes from L.L. Bean, and head off for parts unknown.

- Your parents live considerably longer than anyone, even they, ever thought they would, and they just flat use up every cent they've got.
- Your parents get mad at you and write you out of their will.
- Your parents get mad at your kids and write you out of the will just so there'll be no chance those crummy kids will get their hands on the money.
- Your parents decide you've got a husband who makes a good salary, and because your brother has a lousy job, they change the will so he'll inherit most of their money.

Believe us, again, there are hundreds of scenarios that can topple the best laid plans.

Children are even greater risks. It's a little like buying a lottery ticket. You cannot know how they will choose to live their lives. They may find happiness in a career that pays a lucrative salary, or they may divest themselves of their worldly possessions and enter a monastery.

They may marry or not. They may have no children or ten. They may wipe out their savings on medical costs, housing, disasters, their children's educations, a charity—you can't know. And betting on this is very risky business.

The "Cake"

Do you really want to eat only icing during retirement? Wouldn't you really rather have a cake? If so, you will need to know how to make it.

The Utensils

There are three major points concerning retirement for women:

- Begin your plan as soon as possible.
- Take care of your own plan.
- Become as knowledgeable as possible about your plan.

Begin your Plan ASAP. Begin your plan as soon as you can. Retirement may not be "just around the corner," but the younger you are when you begin, the less expensive it will be for you.

Be aware of the fact that if you begin saving for retirement at age twenty-five, you have forty years of saving ahead of you. If you don't get around to it until you are forty years old, you only have twenty-five years of savings ahead of you. This is a simple concept, but one that is frequently ignored.

Two people trying to arrange the same retirement will have no difficulty in seeing the obvious: It'll be harder to accumulate the same amount of money in twenty-five years than in forty.

In addition, a savings vehicle, such as insurance, will charge less in annual premiums if you are younger. The older you are at the time you purchase the insurance, the more expensive the premium.

Also, keep in mind that if you should begin to save only $5 per month in a retirement account when you are twenty years old, and increase it only when your annual income increases, you more than likely will continue making greater amounts in salary and funneling greater amounts into the retirement savings. The original commitment of only $5 per month at a time when you're not making very much money will not last long. Soon, your earning power will increase, and your commitment to retirement money should increase also.

Let's look at some interesting figures.

If you invested $100 per month beginning at age thirty-five and ending at age sixty-five (thirty years), at the following interest rates, compounded monthly, the results would be quite amazing.

Investment	Interest %	Return
$100	5	$ 83,572
100	10	227,932
100	15	700,982
100	20	2,336,080

We are not suggesting that you wait until you're thirty-five and then start this plan, or that if you've already passed thirty-five you abandon any hope of a comfortable retirement. We are also not suggesting that it's easy to put away $100 per month in a retirement account that earns 20 percent consistently over thirty years. Interest rates vary a great deal; during our lifetimes we have seen them as low as 2 percent and as high as 22 percent. We include these figures so that you'll get some idea that saving realistic amounts of money consistently over the long haul can produce a sum a money that may enable you to stop working at some future date.

Take Care of Your Own Plan. We cannot stress enough the idea that you must consciously decide to be responsible for your own retirement. You put in the money; you get the support.

Be Knowledgeable. Our third point regarding retirement is to be knowledgeable. That may mean that you must become knowledgeable. You may start off knowing and understanding very little. But do whatever you have to do to learn about the various retirement plans available to you. Ask as many questions as you need to. Find someone who can answer your questions in a way that is meaningful to you. Don't be impressed by someone who uses terms that you don't understand. Don't feel you are stupid if you don't get it.

How do you find information about retirement plans? There are several different approaches that you might take. Here are some of the most common:

- If there is a college in your town, it may offer adult education classes in investments and retirement planning. Sometimes such classes are offered also at high schools.
- Consult a certified public accountant (CPA). Accounting firms also offer seminars in investment planning.
- Consult a certified financial planner (CFP). (Look in the phone book for names.)
- Buy magazines on finance, for example, *Money* magazine. They contain advertisements on all types of investing, including retirement. You can call 1-800 numbers to obtain brochures on various investments with no cost and no obligation to you.
- Read financial columns in your daily newspaper.

Unless you're in the business, there is no reason why you would be familiar with financial terms unless you've made it a point to learn about them. A competent financial person will know this and will make it easy for you to understand the options available. An incompetent financial person will try to dazzle you with how much they know, never taking into consideration their primary function—to impart knowledge.

For those of you in domestic partnerships, the important thing to remember is: The time to learn about your retirement plans is not when you're partner dies.

The days when wives are left financially ignorant at the time of their husbands' deaths are not over. Women who never decided to participate in the retirement plan of their partnership leave themselves unaware of the kind of financial shape they are in, and inexperienced in handling money. These pressures, plus the severe emotional trauma of losing a life partner, can be devastating.

Why make it more difficult on yourself than it has to be? Part of being respectful of yourself is always trying to do things that will make your life a little easier, a little less of a struggle. No matter what age you are, make the decision to get actively involved in planning for your retirement.

The Ingredients

The ingredients for this cake we are calling retirement vary from person to person. But, of course, there are some steps that will apply to every woman, such as:

- List your priorities.
- Consider your situation.
- Save regularly.
- Diversify.
- Monitor.
- Get advice.

Priorities. When we say list your priorities, what we mean is simply that retirement means different things to different people. If your desire is to buy an RV and travel all over the country, or spend your last years living in Paris, or stay at home, sleep late, watch lots of TV and read all the books you didn't have time to read while you worked, or take care of all the grandchildren, or raise doberman pinchers—whatever your desires are, that is what you should work toward.

It will be difficult to plan for retirement unless you've got some idea of how you'd best like to spend it. This does not mean you must know positively at age twenty what you'd like to do at age seventy. There is no harm in changing your mind and no harm in changing your financial plans at various points along the way. But it is important to be cognizant of your desires, as much as you can.

Often, retirement plans will include living on a lake, or at the ocean, or in the mountains, or traveling, or buying a boat and fishing, or living in a house that is completely paid for. With plans like these, it helps a great deal to realize your desires early because you can take the necessary financial steps to achieve them.

Considerations. Your situation is unique. And you must make every decision with that awareness. What is good and appropriate for others may not be good and appropriate for you. It takes great courage to go your own way, take the course of action that suits you best (even if it isn't the most popular choice), and follow through on it. But you will feel empowered by those decisions *you choose to make,* and depressed by the decisions that are made for you.

Be realistic about your situation. Do you have parents who will require care? Do you have children, who because of medical or emotional reasons, may never be completely independent of you? Do you have a partner on whom you cannot rely or trust? Do you really want to make the choice to harm yourself financially and perhaps obliterate your chances of retirement altogether in favor of paying for your children's educations?

If you have obligations that you know will continue in later years, please, take them into consideration when you begin to plan. But we urge you to examine each consideration carefully.

Women tend to care for everyone other than themselves, and, as we have said before, are encouraged by society to do so. If your son could work and put himself through college, allowing you to put away retirement money, would you really choose to spend your money on tuition bills? If your parents could choose to sell the gigantic house they're living in and have a lavish retirement, is it really appropriate for you to bankrupt yourself caring for them? If they're making financial choices they and you know are clearly not in their best interest, at what point does your obligation to them outweigh your care for yourself?

These are hard questions sometimes because emotions run very high where family obligations are concerned. And nowhere in families do emotions run higher than when women begin to have their own agendas. Usually, every member of the family will simultaneously shout, "We liked everything much better the other way!"

So don't be surprised if your decisions, or even your questions, are greeted by surprise, horror, hostility, or an out-and-out fit. Trust us. Everyone will live through your adulthood. They may not enjoy the process very much, but they'll survive it, and they'll survive their own growing up process too.

Save Regularly. We simply cannot say this often enough. And if you take only one point from all of these pages, let it be this one: *Save regularly!*

Saving money is probably the most important step you can take to financial autonomy, to the availability of choices, to good decision-making, to empowerment.

Once you've determined what you'd like to retire to, and what considerations you will have to deal with, it's time to begin to sock that money away. Once you've got your monthly plan up and running, it should be easy to determine, from the money you have left, how much will go into retirement savings.

Financial experts have suggested percentages of 10 percent to 20 percent of your annual income, and higher if you want to take early retirement. And while those are certainly figures to aspire to (and we think the higher the better), those are not figures that are meant to be obstacles.

In other words, if you look at your current situation and you know for a fact that you can only afford to put 3 percent of your income into retirement, don't be discouraged by the fact that it's only 3 percent. The important thing here is to start saving—the percentage doesn't matter. You can increase it with determination as time goes on, but you can't increase something you haven't started.

So start saving! Right away!

Diversify. As we discussed in the savings chapter, we highly encourage diversification of funds. It is never wise to have all your retirement money in one account, one bank, one insurance company, one anything. Spread it around. Take advantage of different accounts, different banks, different companies.

Monitor. Monitor your plans. This is extremely important. Watch your money! Don't just shovel money into a plan for ninety years without reading your statements, reading the newspaper, and keeping up with the general condition of the economic world and your plan in particular.

Don't panic! We're not asking that you become an economic expert, start subscribing to all kinds of money magazines, take the *Wall Street Journal,* and have power lunches. Please do all of those things if you want to—but don't feel that they're necessary. It is merely necessary that you keep well enough apprised so you don't make uninformed choices.

Get Advice. While we whole-heartedly advocate making your own decisions, we do not ever suggest that you make them without the tools or information necessary to insure their wisdom. In retirement, as in everything else, visit with an expert. Consult a CPA. Consult a financial planner. Speak to a banker. Speak to an insurance agent. Go to your library and check out books on financial programs before pursuing them in your personal plan. Talk to friends and family to get their opinions.

Always know up front, however, that the ultimate decision will and should rest with you. You will have no one else to credit and no one to blame. The decisions you make will be entirely your own. If they arise out of a thorough search for information, rather than from a motivation of fear or apathy, they will give you confidence and strengthen your feelings of self-esteem daily.

How to Bake Your Cake

Prior to the days when there were IRAs (Individual Retirement Accounts), people simply saved and saved for later years. They hoped they could put away enough in the mattress, in the coffee can, in the bank savings account, to take them through the last years of their lives and have enough left over to give them a proper burial. There might even be some left over for the kids, but that was asking a lot.

Believe it or not, there was actually a time when the phrase "pre-tax" dollars was unheard of because all dollars were "pre-tax" when there was no tax. Putting money away these days, though, is slightly more complicated. Income tax is a big consideration. The federal government can encourage or discourage saving by taxing savings and retirement accounts or by not taxing them. When you choose a retirement plan, know what the tax aspects of the plan are.

The primary types of retirement plans are IRAs, SEPs, and 401-Ks. Let's look at each of them.

IRAs. Individual Retirement Accounts are very flexible retirement plans, and the money in an IRA can be invested in a variety of ways. The typical IRA opened by an ordinary person is a fund that you contribute to regularly (you don't have to, but you should) and that continually earns interest, both on your contributions and on the interest already accrued. It's as easy to open them as it is to open a bank account, so don't hesitate a minute to open an IRA!

These are accounts that you voluntarily fund, with an amount of your choice, which you may increase, decrease or freeze at any time. You may withdraw the money, but there is a substantial tax penalty attached to early withdrawal—and early withdrawal means "before retirement age."

If you want to change your IRA, you may "roll it over" to another IRA account without a tax penalty so long as it is done within sixty days after you take it out of the first IRA. Tax laws can change in the future though, so keep up with them.

You may open an IRA at a bank, an insurance company, or a financial firm (such as a stock brokerage house). Because this is money you will not expect to see for several years, even though you will want to monitor its activities carefully, you will also want to invest in institutions with good reputations that are managed conservatively and in which you feel confident.

Two wonderful qualities of IRAs are: (1) You may be able to deduct the first $2,000 of your contribution from your taxable income; and (2) The interest earned on an IRA account is tax-deferred, which means that it is taxed when you receive it in retirement, not the year it is earned. Not everyone is entitled to deduct the $2,000 a year, however. Whether you can take this deduction depends on your income level and whether your company has a pension plan. By being able to deduct the amount of IRA dollars you have contributed in one year from your taxable income, and by being able to defer paying tax on the interest earned until retirement, you actually reduce your taxable income in the present.

In other words, and let's use hypothetical numbers here because the laws change frequently, suppose your taxable income were $24,000 and the tax on that amount was $4,200. If you had contributed $2,000 to an IRA, that $2,000 would simply be deducted from your income of $24,000, making your taxable income now only $22,000. The tax on $22,000 would be approximately $3,640.

As you can see, along with putting away $2,000 toward your retirement, and not including the interest earned as part of your income, you would also save $560 ($4,200 − $3,640) in the present in taxes. It might be helpful to note here that your income is lowered by $1,440, not really $2,000, because of the $560 tax savings.

SEPs. SEP stands for "simplified employee pension plan." If you have income from self-employment, you may pay a certain amount of it into a SEP plan. It is very similar to an IRA. The contribution will be deducted from your income, so the contribution will be in pre-tax dollars. Also, the income earned by whatever investment you have chosen will not be taxed in the year it is earned, but only when you have retired and taken the money out.

401-Ks. Those of you who work for companies may be offered a 401-K. This is also an excellent option and one that you should think seriously about contributing to. Companies will normally match employee contributions in these plans at varying percentages up to 100 percent, dollar for dollar. This is unbeatable. These plans are tax-deferred, and when you leave the company, this money can be returned to you if you wish. You then have the opportunity to "roll it over" into another IRA account without penalty or tax. (NOTE: If you take this money and don't roll it over, it becomes part of your income for that year and you will have to pay income tax on it.)

Pre-Tax versus Post-Tax. Let us tell you up front. In this battle, pre-tax always wins. For those of you who have heard this phrase but never quite knew what it meant, this is it.

Any plan that allows you to contribute pre-tax dollars is letting you contribute to the plan before your income level is assessed for tax. If your company offers you a plan that takes pre-tax dollars, and you contribute to the plan, your income is reduced by the amount of your contribution. Because your income is lower, the amount of tax you pay is also lower.

Let's be more specific. If the government takes $540 out of your $1,800 paycheck, that leaves you with a take-home pay of $1,260. If you contribute $100 to a pre-tax retirement plan, that reduces your $1,800 paycheck to $1,700. The government's tax on $1,700 will be less than it is on $1,800. Instead of $540, it might be closer to $510—this would be a savings to you of $30 in each paycheck.

This same scenario in post-tax dollars goes like this. Your check is $1,800, the government reduces that by $540, leaving you $1,260; from that $1,260, you contribute your $100, leaving you with $1,160.

	Post-tax	**Pre-tax**
Income	$1800	$1800
	- 540 (tax)	- 100 (contr.)
Subtotal	$1260	$1700
	- 100 (contr.)	- 510 (tax)
Take-Home	$1160	$1190

This is how the battle is won. You keep more of your money, less goes to taxes, and you contribute to your own retirement in the process.

Any time you're eligible for such a plan, take advantage of it. Educators usually are offered a tax-deferred retirement annuity by their school or college. Many times, the school will also contribute to this plan in behalf of the teacher. These are normally pre-tax dollar, tax-deferred interest, and conservatively managed plans. They are an excellent option for those of you who teach.

Insurance. We discussed insurance at length in an earlier chapter, but we'd like to reiterate here that, depending on what you're trying to accomplish financially, you may invest in some form of insurance with retirement in mind. Most insurance companies also offer IRAs. Again, be sure that you're dealing with a reputable company and with an agent who treats you with respect. Go to the library and ask the reference librarian for help in locating a highly-rated insurance company.

Conclusion

Retirement planning is part of the total package of care you choose to provide yourself. It is a conscious choice, consciously and conscientiously executed by you, in your own behalf. What may be right for others may not be right for you, but doing exactly what *is* right for you will give you strength and confidence.

The ultimate goal of retirement planning is the ability to choose: "Can I choose to stop working or can't I?"

The choice, at least in part, is in your hands. We say, in part, because we do take into account the existence or absence of luck, the myriad of possibilities surrounding world economy as we know it, and the way the stars line up. But, short of those uncontrollables, we really believe that you have the power to affect your own life and to see to it that you enjoy the ability to choose throughout your days.

Savings and retirement plans are designed to build up the *asset* side of your financial picture. The next chapter, credit, deals with the *liability* side.

CHAPTER EIGHT

Credit

About 50 percent of our clients felt emphatically that credit was a curse. The other 50 percent felt that they'd be dead today if it hadn't been for credit. They all spoke with great conviction and with years of experience behind them. Many of you reading this book may feel as strongly on one side or the other.

But, just as we've been doing throughout this book, we'd like once again to point out the difference between the myth and the reality. We want to give you a new perspective on credit that includes the ever important concept of balance.

Some of you probably turned to this chapter first because you are in a credit crunch, and you feel like it's killing you. Others just need good information about how to balance the use of credit with the other aspects of your plan. Some readers will be looking for basic information about credit. This chapter will offer all types of information.

First, we will talk about what credit is, the function of credit in our society, and credit reports as profiles of each of us in society. Then we will distinguish between credit in balance, which is credit we control and use to our advantage, and credit out of balance, which is debt that has grown until it seems to control us. We will discuss how to get out of a credit crunch. Finally, we will demonstrate some deadly credit traps many women fall into, and give a word of advice on using credit in a self-owned business.

What Is Credit?

Let's begin by defining credit. Credit is a legal financial agreement. A company or institution extends you credit by lending you money outright, allowing you to purchase goods, or allowing you to access money at your convenience up to a certain amount. The company then expects you to repay that money, usually in monthly installments (but the time frame may vary), and with a particular percentage of interest assessed on the unpaid portion of the debt.

What this means is that you become the borrower and the bank that issues the credit card or the retail store that issues the charge card becomes the lender. You pay the lender interest for the privilege of borrowing the money.

Credit is neutral; it is not evil and it is not good. There is no need to "avoid it like the plague" or to "make it your life." There are no hard-and-fast rules about credit. But, let's get one thing straight up front: credit is debt. Sit for a moment and let that concept sink in. It's not a bad concept, but it is one of those very realistic facts that become lost in the numerous credit myths that are generated by our society. When you use credit, in any form, you are putting yourself in debt.

And debt, like all things, must be balanced, and must be entered into with awareness. There is no difference between charging a tank of gasoline with your gasoline credit card, and charging a television on your Visa, or borrowing $5,000 from the bank. The dollar amounts and the interest rates vary, but the concept is precisely the same. You have obligated yourself through credit to repay a debt at a later date.

Credit cards are not windfalls. If you will recall, we discussed windfalls in the income chapter. We are looking at windfalls again now because the strangest concept came to light in our counseling sessions: the concept that new credit cards are windfalls.

Au contraire! Credit is a method to incur debt. It is nothing else. If you get a new credit card in the mail and it says the limit is $5,000, that does not mean that you now have $5,000 in assets. It means that you now have the ability to borrow $5,000 and become obligated for its payback. It is a debt vehicle, *not* an asset in any way.

The Function of Credit in Our Society

It's no doubt apparent to all of you that our society is geared toward credit transactions. A person trying to function on a totally cash basis will be asked a lot of seemingly stupid questions.

Small plastic credit cards virtually flood the nation. Visas, MasterCards, American Express, an endless number of retail store charge cards, telephone cards, ATM (automatic teller machine) cards, and Discover are a convenience and a source of ready cash.

Society loves credit. And by society we mean the majority of businesses and people. There is one very simple reason for this: instant gratification.

By offering credit, businesses have the gratification of many sales. Unfortunately, they frequently sell themselves out of business, which means that they have very high sales, all on credit that rarely gets paid back. The myth is that if you're working hard and pushing lots of inventory or services out the door in the form of sales, then it doesn't matter whether those sales are credit sales or cash sales.

It does matter. It matters a great deal. Credit sales are not income until they are paid. And credit sales that are never paid or only partially paid equal a loss.

We are not suggesting that businesses should return to strictly cash and carry methods. But we did want to point out the reason credit is so pervasive in our society. Making the product as easy to purchase as possible is the best way to insure higher sales. As far as the sales department is concerned, what could be easier than a plastic card? Once the sale goes bad, it becomes the problem of an entirely different department (the credit or collection department).

Like businesses, people love instant gratification. Speed is a high priority in our society when it comes to purchasing ability. It is a very low priority when it comes to paying for the purchases. Let's say you're starting a new job that pays $20,000 per year. Do you instantly go out and spend several hundred dollars on clothing for the new job, or do you wear what you have until you're sure the job will work out? Do you set aside money on a monthly basis and buy clothes as you are able?

Most individuals give absolutely no thought to charging several hundreds of dollars worth of clothing when they start a new job that is paying them an annual salary of $20,000. Let's look at what happens to them as a result of their need for instant gratification. After taxes and social security (FICA), they may actually take home $14,000 in a year. After they pay their fixed expenses, they *may* be left with $4,500 for controllables (food, entertainment, clothing) for the year. That's $375 per month from which they plan to pay all their controllables plus the debt for the clothing. Wait! Consider balance! Be aware! Examine your priorities!

Credit Reports as Profiles of Each of Us

As many of you probably know, credit reporting is a fairly big business. There are central credit reporting agencies in every state with massive data bases. This information is easily transferred daily via telephone and computer from one place to another. Our society is geared toward credit, and the record keeping that goes with your personal credit file is tremendous.

For those of you who have never seen your personal credit file, we strongly suggest that you order a copy from your local credit-reporting agency. There will be a charge of $10 or more, depending on where you live. You will need to show identification and may, perhaps, need to sign for the copy, but it is your right to obtain a copy of your file.

The reason you might want to obtain a copy is that it's good to see what everyone else sees when you apply for credit of any kind. Each time you fill out an application for a credit card, a retail charge card, a gasoline card, a loan, a car, or a mortgage the institution from which you are attempting to borrow the money orders a copy of your credit file.

If you have a common last name, have been divorced, or are married to a partner whose credit is in poor condition, you will especially want to obtain a copy of this report.

We had one client whose last name was a common name. We'll call her Smith. She attempted to buy a car and was turned down because the bank reported that her credit file contained several liens and judgments against her. It turned out that that information belonged to another Smith who coincidentally had the same first name. The only way the credit reporting agency was able to differentiate the information was by social security number. Her file was corrected and updated at that time so the problem would not continue.

A typical credit report will contain the following information:

- name
- address
- place of employment
- date of birth
- social security number
- a listing of current creditors:
    1. *opening date of the account*
    2. *highest balance (high credit extended)*
    3. *current balance*
    4. *times delinquent*
    5. *overall pay rating*
- a listing of companies or institutions that have inquired about the individual's credit
- suits
- liens
- judgments

Much of this information will be difficult for the inexperienced person to read because it will be in credit code. But there are explanations of the codes on the back of the report, and the credit-reporting agency employees will be happy to translate your report for you.

Credit in Balance

Because credit is the method we use to incur debt, there are several general rules that apply to all credit transactions. While the specifics will vary from transaction to transaction, the basic rules will not change, so we will highlight some of those for you.

Credit Philosophy

Credit is based on the philosophy of using someone else's money to accomplish a desired task and then repaying the lender according to terms that it sets down in its lending agreement. And, contrary to myth, lending agreements are not always long, tiny typed volumes of small print handed to you by bankers wearing green eye-shades. Whether you realize it or not, each time you sign a charge slip, a credit application, a cash advance bank slip, or a promissory note, you are signing a lending agreement that is every bit as binding as the small print the banker hands you.

Using someone else's money rather than your own is often a very wise choice, particularly if that choice is made with the awareness of how incurring the debt will affect your financial condition.

Credit in the Plan

The philosophy of our plan is to emphasize three things: balance, awareness, and choice. It is necessary to have a balanced attitude toward credit, not to view it from the extremes of evil or good; to be aware each time you obligate yourself to debt through credit; to be aware of the role debt is playing in your life; and finally, to be honest about your own personal choices where credit is concerned.

Let us give you a few examples. We saw one client who spent several years working out of a very heavy debt situation. When she was finally at a debt-free place in her finances, her car bit the dust and it was imperative to shop for a new one. She had built up her assets to a place where, if she were to drain all of her savings, she would probably have been able to buy a modestly priced car for cash. She toyed with this idea for quite some time, because the idea of signing a note to finance the purchase of the car was more than she felt she could bear. We cautioned her about balance. Would it make good financial sense to deplete her assets entirely rather than finance a car when she had no other debts? Of course not. She settled eventually on a nice compromise. She used a portion of her assets to make a downpayment on the car and financed the rest.

Another client decided to stop using her credit cards altogether in an attempt to bring a halt to her increasing debt. She began to make larger monthly payments on the existing debt as part of her plan to pay everything off. However, she still felt she could not function without a credit card. So she applied for and received a new Visa and began to use it, never really thinking that she was shooting herself in the financial foot by continuing to incur debt on the new Visa, even though she was allocating very large amounts of money toward the old debt. Clearly, she made these decisions without credit awareness.

We counseled one client who became the prime example in our discussion of personal choices. This woman was doing wonderfully well with her money; in fact, she was seeing us under protest. She rented an apartment, had a good job that she truly enjoyed, made a decent salary, and chose to incur a moderate debt by travelling. She had been all over the world and was one of our most interesting clients. The reason she made the appointment was that she had been receiving quite a bit of pressure from friends and family to settle down and buy a house. She felt that she couldn't afford a house and so had come to a session, secretly hoping that we would confirm her feelings.

Financially, she had adequate income to buy a house, but not if she wanted to continue to travel, and she did want to continue to travel—more than anything. Everyone she knew gave her all kinds of reasons why she was stupid to rent when she could own a house. But her personal priorities were quite clear. She had no desire to own a house, to care for a house, to do yardwork, to pay real estate taxes, and to acquire all the rest of the obligations that go with being a homeowner. For her, the debt she incurred on travel *was* debt that she was happy to repay. Any other kind of debt would have felt very burdensome. Needless to say, we supported her decision to continue traveling rather than to become a homeowner.

These clients were all best served by keeping in mind the three principles of balance, awareness and choice as they made their credit decisions.

The Credit Catch—When to Use Credit

The catch where credit is concerned is when to use it. Credit should be used when you don't need to use it. We know that sounds crazy on the first reading, so we'll try to explain.

That doesn't mean that if you need a car you shouldn't finance it. It doesn't mean that you should only sign a mortgage to buy a house when you don't want one. What we mean here is that it is important to keep credit available to you. It is imperative to have access to ready means of credit. You will only be in this position if you use your credit wisely.

For example, if you have two Visas, both with credit limits of $2,000, you have a total of $4,000 available credit. If you charge $4,000 (both cards to the limit), you have eliminated your access to funds. At that point, you have no available credit and a debt that needs to be taken care of. You are essentially "stuck."

But by incurring a moderate amount of debt, keeping your credit lines open and available, and repaying the debt at amounts that are not burdensome to you, you will always have the credit when you need it, and the choices that go along with that.

Choose Your Debts

Credit takes on many different faces, but it is always incurring debt. The terms of the indebtedness are always set by the lender, whether it's a retail store, a bank, a credit union, or a bank-issued credit card. You need to know the terms of whatever debt you incur so that you'll meet your financial obligations on time.

It is also important to understand the terms because you always have choices, and you may not like the terms of one credit card but may find another credit card that suits your income and financial condition better. For example, you may be using a Visa that charges 19.5 percent interest plus an annual fee of $25. Why would you knowingly choose to keep this Visa if you could obtain one with a 13 percent interest rate and no annual fee? The answer is that you would not *knowingly* make that choice, but you might have made it *unknowingly*. And that's what we'd like to see you change.

Terms vary to a great degree, and that's why it's very important to shop around—in every instance from the biggest mortgage to the smallest credit purchase. Terms always include three components: (1) a dollar limit, (2) an interest rate, and (3) a time frame.

To illustrate, we're going to set up a hypothetical situation and show you how drastic the effects of not shopping around can be.

Let's look at a typical mortgage, which is perhaps the greatest amount of credit that is ever extended to most of us. Let's suppose that two people buy houses that are priced at $75,000.

Person A applies for a mortgage without any awareness of the effects of mortgage terms. She secures a mortgage at 12 percent for thirty years, for $75,000. Her monthly payment is $771.46. (For simplification, we are leaving out real estate taxes and insurance, which would be added to this amount.)

Person B applies for a mortgage for $75,000 and after shopping around gets one for 9 percent interest for thirty years. Her monthly payment is only $603.47.

Let's say there is a Person C, who wants to secure the same mortgage at 9% but wants it for only fifteen years. Her monthly payment would be only $760.70.

As you can see, if person A could have found the mortgage that Person C found, she would have owned the house in half the time, saved $10.76 per month ($129.12 per year) on the house payments, and paid considerably less interest.

Please do not underestimate the importance of the terms of credit, and don't be afraid to shop around until you find terms that are reasonable and suit your financial condition. This is a good time to review what you presently have and examine such things as the terms of your credit indebtedness, the balances, the due dates, and the cut-off dates just to familiarize yourself with your own situation. You can't make good decisions if you don't have all the facts.

For those of you interested in a general survey of the credit cards available to you, their interest rates, their annual fees (if any), and the options they provide, we suggest you send $14.95 to an organization called "Consumer Credit Card Rating Service" located at Post Office Box 5219, Santa Monica, California 90405. This company will send you a package that surveys all the available credit cards across the country. You may find a much better deal than the one you have.

Considerations

The Beauty of Thirty Days. Interest on purchases made with most credit and charge cards does not begin to accrue until the due date passes and the balance on the account has not been paid. Further, most credit cards and charge cards run on a thirty-day billing cycle. This means that you may have the use of someone else's money for thirty days or more, interest-free.

However, some lenders begin to charge interest from the date of the purchase. Be sure to read the lending agreement on the back of your monthly statement to find out exactly which type of account you have.

If the terms of your card give you an interest-free thirty days, you may have the use of the lender's money for nearly sixty days without any cost to you if you do a small amount of advance planning. Check on your statement so you will know what the billing cut-off date is. Now check to see what the due date is. If the billing date and the due date are the same, you can have a full sixty days to pay your bill interest-free. If the billing date and due date are different, then the maximum number of interest-free days available to you will be thirty days plus the number of days between the billing date and the due date.

For example, if the billing date is the 10th and the due date is the 30th of each month, by making a purchase on the 11th, you have just given yourself fifty days in which to pay your bill without incurring interest. By making your purchases as close to the day after the 10th as possible you give yourself the maximum number of days available to you.

Suppose the cut-off date on your credit card is the 10th, the due date is the 10th, and it's now the 11th of January. If you make a purchase today, that purchase will not show up on your statement until the 10th of February and you will have until the 10th of March to pay for it without incurring any interest (finance charges). So, an item you bought on January 11th with someone else's money will not actually be paid until slightly before March 10th—nearly 60 days.

More on Using Someone Else's Money. The due dates and cut-off dates of credit accounts are very important because, by being aware of them, you can time your purchases and your payments to fit into your plan. Let's see how.

Imagine, for example, that your MasterCard has a billing cut-off date of the 10th and a payment due date of the 25th. This means that the lender expects you to pay your bill by the 25th, and the monthly statement that is sent out will contain all transactions up to the 10th of the given month.

If you're working within your plan, you've got your debt under control, and decide that you have approximately $50 extra per month to spend on anything you want, you might want to review your options. You could take $50 in cash out of your account every month and spend the cash money on the items of your choice, or you could use your credit card up to $50 every month and pay it in full when it comes in.

There are a couple of advantages to using your credit card so we'll spell them out right here: (1) You will be using someone else's money; and (2) You will be contributing to a good credit rating for yourself, which will become part of your permanent credit history.

If you are unsure exactly how much you can charge per month, or you know that each month is different, an easy method to use is this: Each time you use your credit card, write out a check for that amount and put it in an envelope. You will begin to see your checking-account balance in the check register decrease. At some point, you will feel that it is uncomfortably low, and you will know that it is time for you to stop incurring debt for that month. When the credit card statement arrives, simply gather up the checks you have written, which you've kept in an envelope for that purpose, and mail all of them with your bill. The credit card company doesn't care whether you pay your bill with one check or ten, so long as you pay it.

Interest Rates. An interest rate on a debt is the charge that is assessed on the unpaid portion of whatever you owe. There are laws that regulate the percentage of interest that can be charged, and these laws vary from state to state. When an institution charges an amount of interest that exceeds the legal rate, it is called usury, and it is a crime for which the victim has legal recourse.

Even though there is a legal limit on interest, rates still vary a great deal within the same state, as each institution tries its best to recruit customers. Consequently, there may be ten major banks in your city, each one offering a Visa or MasterCard, and each one offering a different rate of interest. The differences may be only slight, but we hope that you can see what a small difference in interest can make.

For example, if you had a Visa that assessed 15 percent interest and you bought an item that cost $1,000, in one year you would have paid $150 in interest, so that item would actually have cost you $1,150.

If you bought the same item with a Visa that charged only 10 percent interest, the cost would decrease to $1,100, saving you $50.

If you paid the item off in three months, the first Visa would have charged you $1,037.50. The second Visa would have cost only $1,025.

No matter how you calculate it, the interest rate makes a big difference that affects you *directly*. It is the difference between keeping money or losing money. But you must become aware of these differences before you can do anything about them.

Annual Fees. Annual fees of $10 or more are assessed on many, but not all, credit cards. The purpose of annual fees is for the lender to make money—very simple.

A credit card may come with a wide array of services, such as travel insurance, hotel discounts, rental car accommodations, or life insurance to justify the fact that the issuing company is charging its customers an annual fee of $30, in addition to interest. However, the truth is, a very small percentage of the customers actually use the available options, while all the customers pay for them.

There are cards available that do not assess annual fees, and, if that suits your lifestyle better, we suggest you pay off the credit card you're using and switch to one that is more compatible with your money-management plan.

Credit out of Balance—the Credit Crunch

If you are among the 50 percent of people who feel that credit is sometimes a curse, this is the section you've been waiting for. How do I get out of a credit crunch? This is the most commonly asked question in any counseling session we've ever had.

Most of the clients who come to us are in debt situations that are out of control. But once they formulate their plans, they take control of those debts, and they stop feeling as though the debts are controlling them. Feeling that your debts have control over you is the credit crunch.

How to get out of that crunch becomes the million-dollar question.

How to Eliminate Debt

There are two ways to eliminate debt: Pay it off, or go bankrupt.

You may see countless advertisements trying to sell you a zillion different ways out of bad financial situations. But the facts are these. You either pay the debt, or you take what is known as Chapter 7 bankruptcy and have all your debts discharged (eliminated). Do not even consider bankruptcy until you have read this chapter.

The Plan

Our plan does not assume that you wish to repay your debts. It encourages you throughout the book to do what's right for you. Review your options. Make good choices with your best interest at heart. It may be that bankruptcy is the process you'd like to begin, or it may be that repaying your debts suits you better in every way.

What we can tell you is this: If you choose to repay your debts, we will show you the most efficient way to do so that is the least burdensome to you. We will show you how to get out of this credit crunch you're in and turn your life around.

We can show you. But, the truth is, it is you who must do it. And it is hard work, although our plan will make it a little easier than it might have been otherwise.

Getting Out of the Crunch

Let's assume that you'd like to repay your debts. No matter how you originally came to have those debts, there are certain factors to consider when making the decision to pay them off.

- Examine your existing debts:
    1. *Check the balances owed.*
    2. *Make a note of the interest rates.*
    3. *Keep in mind if there is any available credit.*
    4. *Check the amount of the monthly payment.*
- Total your existing debts and compare that figure with the total of your existing assets.
- Add the total monthly minimum payments to see how much money you are allocating to debt reduction at present.
- Rank your debts in order from lowest balance to highest balance.
- Check for any available sources of credit.
- Begin the process of consolidation.
- Contact your creditors.

For the sake of clarity, we will present a hypothetical situation.

Let's say we have a client whose debt condition is as follows:

Debtor	Balance	Int. Rate	Pmt.	Credit Lmt.
Visa	$2500	15%	$ 50	$5,000
MC	1000	13%	35	1,200
Sears	376	12%	15	1,000
Dentist	125	8%	25	
Plumber	400	10%	100	
St. Loan	900	5%	62	
Doctor	97	10%	25	

When we total this existing debt, we find that the complete indebtedness equals $5,398.

When we total the existing monthly payments, we find that they equal $312.

When we rank the debts in order from smallest to largest, they rank as follows:

Debtor	Balance
Doctor	$ 97
Dentist	125
Sears	376
Plumber	400
Student loan	900
MC	1000
Visa	2500

When we look for available sources of credit, we check first with the existing debt, and we find that the Visa has a balance of $2,500 and a credit limit of $5,000, an available credit amount of $2,500.

There is no other available credit among existing debt. We then look to other sources, such as other credit lines available to the client that she is not currently using, any money owed to her, and any assets that she has. Believe it or not, many clients have ample savings to pay off the debts that plague them and still retain a secure amount in savings, but they feel that they should not use any of their savings.

In this example, we don't have to look very far. The available credit of $2,500 will solve most of her problems without costing her additional money, saving our client a great deal.

With the available credit line of $2,500 on the Visa, she will obtain a cash advance of $1,998 with which she will pay off the doctor, the dentist, Sears, the plumber, and MasterCard. The reason we did not counsel paying off the student loan is that the interest rate of 5 percent is so much lower than the interest rate of 13 percent on the MasterCard that it made better sense to rid our client of the more expensive debt.

This also rids the client of five monthly payments totaling $200. So, without spending a cent or going to the bank, we have reallocated her total debt. The client still owes $5,398, but now she can begin to pay it back with a little more breathing room. Her monthly payments now total only $112 plus the increased amount on the Visa balance. For the sake of this example, we will estimate that the Visa monthly payment will increase to $125 with the increased balance.

It is very important that you check the terms of your particular card. Some cards schedule their monthly payment as a percentage of the balance, some as maximum and minimum amounts, some in accordance with an existing schedule of payments.

In our example, instead of paying $312 per month to seven debts, she now has only two bills to pay, which total approximately $187 ($62 + $125), her student loan and her Visa. With the money she has freed up by paying off the smaller bills, she can now reallocate that money to the Visa and the Student Loan. In fact, if she took that money and paid the student loan, it would be paid off in approximately seven months, and then the entire $312 could be used aggressively to attack the Visa, which would be her only debt.

This would be the way our chart would look now:

Debtor	Balance	Rate	Payment
Student Loan	$ 900	5%	$ 62 / month
Visa	4498	15%	125 / month
Total	$5398		$187 / month

Having debt that is strapping you is not fun. But getting rid of debt, once you make your mind up to do so, does not have to be an awful experience.

Now, obviously, you will sabotage your own plan if you continue to aggressively acquire new debt while you are aggressively attacking your existing debt. This is a spiral that cannot end well and will keep your anxiety level at record heights. We are not advocating that you run out, get cash advances on every Visa you can lay your hands on, and run it up to the max! You must make up your mind that debt will not control you; you will control it. And then, you begin, one by one, to eliminate your debts in the best way possible for you.

A common question we are asked is this: "The Visa charges the highest rate of interest. Why would we want to use it for our available source of credit?"

The answer is not complicated. If our client had another, less expensive source of credit, we'd use it. But, the assumption we made in this example is that, short of going to a bank and applying for a loan (which she'd probably have trouble getting because of her debt condition), and short of applying for another credit card, the existing Visa seemed like the best option, even at 15 percent.

In addition, it's important to weigh all the factors, not just base your decision on one. The reduction in monthly payments of approximately $125 ($312 – $187) is a good reason for the actions we took. There was no chance of eliminating the Visa debt, which would be the ideal option, and so working with it and letting it help her was the next best thing.

We'd like to make one final suggestion concerning the last point on page 162: "contact your creditors." The most destructive thing you can do if you are saddled with overwhelming debt is to deny it. The most empowering thing you can do is to handle it. And handling it requires that you contact, either by phone or letter, the lenders to whom you owe money and explain your situation to them thoroughly: Tell them (don't ask them) exactly what you intend to do about it. Lenders panic when they don't hear from borrowers. They don't panic when they do. And we have run across very few lenders who preferred to litigate rather than try everything imaginable to work out the debt situation with the borrower, providing, of course, that the borrower calls, always tells the truth, keeps promises, and has a plan.

Credit Traps

All individuals can and do fall into credit traps at times in their lives. For women, the workplace seems to be particularly dangerous for many reasons. The two credit traps we have seen most frequently are the clothes trap and the "front money" trap.

The Clothes Trap

The greatest credit trap for women in the workplace has to do with clothes. And while many people, men and women, have a penchant for clothes, that is not what we're discussing here. Let's look at the scenario.

An executive vice-president (usually male) of a fairly large company is paid a salary of $125,000 annually and receives an annual bonus based on profitability and access to company stock through options. In addition, the company squirrels away a tidy little pension for him.

This man hires a secretary, whose job it will be to manage all the clerical demands of his position, accompany him to meetings, at times travel with him, and in general, look very appropriate as she stands by his side when they meet other people. She is paid an annual salary of perhaps $25,000 (for most parts of the country we're being generous here)—that's it. No bonus, no stock options, and a pension only if every other person in the entire organization is paid one.

The credit trap here is how does this woman buy appropriate clothes on her salary?

There is only one answer to this. She goes into debt. She charges her credit cards to their maximum limits in an attempt to look the female counterpart of her very appropriately dressed boss, who is squeaking by on $100,000 more than she is.

In many cases, the female employee is also raising children—alone. So, now let's spread that $25,000 a year over one or two children.

The most amazing fact about this scenario, which we saw so frequently it was shocking, is that these women don't become insolvent more quickly than they do. They are in impossible financial situations, and the fact that they hang on as long as they do before insolvency becomes an issue that must be faced is a credit to their remarkably good use of the little they have.

The irony is, of course, that the female employee has no bigger critics about her supposedly poor money-managing skills than the boss and the rest of male management. If she, in fact, decides that bankruptcy is her only option, she is very likely to find management completely unsympathetic to her need for time off to attend court hearings, attorney consultations, etc.

Office clothes can become your biggest credit trap, and purchasing these clothes may be one of the most financially destructive activities you ever engage in.

We again suggest balance. Don't do something that is not in your best interest financially for the sake of fulfilling someone else's expectations of you. You only need to fulfill your own expectations, and you may find that that will cost surprisingly little in comparison. It is unreasonable for anyone to expect you to dress in a way that you cannot afford. You cannot be expected to make purchases on a regular basis that exceed your income for the sake of keeping that income. It's irrational.

What is a solution to this trap? We suggest several solutions.

- Buy several suits and blouses and interchange them.
- Don't take a job that requires you to spend more money on your clothes than you can afford.
- Take the job, wear clothes you can afford, and when management criticizes your appearance, tell them to pay you more money. They're certain to like your clothes better after that!
- Tell your boss you don't like his clothes, either.

(We're only partly joking about the last two solutions.)

The "Front-Money" Trap

Another common credit trap that plagues women in the workplace is what we call "front money."

Front money is when you, as an employee, are expected to perform some duty (take a trip, make a purchase, take a client to dinner) and use your own money. Of course, the company promises to reimburse you and in almost every case, it does. But that isn't the point. There is a difference between employer money and employee money, and you should *never* use your money when it is the obligation of the employer to pay.

We actually had one client who was very much into her plan, and doing very well. She was strapped for money and had a heavy debt load that she was chipping away at, little by little. She was in public relations, and one of her jobs was to visit other firms frequently and make presentations about her firm. This was not a once-in-a-while activity; this was a job she performed at least three days a week.

Many of the firms she visited were in her state, and she traveled by car (her own) and frequently had to spend the night if the company was too far from her home.

One of her big complaints was that she was expected to front the money for the trips, which included gas, hotels, meals, and client dinners. The reimbursement process was extraordinarily slow, to make matters worse, and she had no available credit cards because she had put a stop to debt as part of her plan. Being determined that her plan should succeed, she resented the idea that the company was asking her to come up with money she did not have.

One of her bosses actually yelled at her for not keeping her credit card lines open and available so she wouldn't cause such a problem for the company.

Wait a minute! Hold on! Please! If you are in this position, get out of it this minute!

We don't mean that you should quit your job. But we do mean to tell you that there is no reason why you, as an employee, should be expected or feel obligated to provide funds for the company to run on. That is essentially what you are doing. If the company does not have the funds to run its normal day-to-day activities, then you had probably better quit because at some point in the near future your paycheck will probably not be worth too much.

We urge you not to be the care-taker. Be courageous. Walk into your boss's office and explain that you'll be delighted to go on the trip, or to take that client to dinner, or to purchase those needed items, just as soon as you have some money. It can be in the form of an advance, or in the form of a company credit card. Assure your boss that you'll return all the receipts, file any expense reports needed, and justify every penny you spend, but you will no longer use your own money as operating capital for the company.

Recognize abuse when you see it. Well-run companies do not require their employees to front money, because they realize that it is abusive behavior. It is abusive to make someone else pay your bills. You would be outraged if you went out to dinner with two people who both left the table promptly before the waiter brought the check, leaving you to pay for it. It is no less abusive when companies do this. Let them call the practice whatever they want, but you make sure you know it for what it is—financial abuse.

Self-Employment

We wanted to say a little something about self-employment because one of the biggest pitfalls we found for clients who came to see us was this: mixing personal and business charges.

By all means, if you own a business, no matter how big or small, please do everything you can to keep your business transactions separate from your personal transactions.

In other words, be sure to maintain a business checking account, a business savings account, and business credit cards. And be very vigilant about using business credit cards for business expenses and personal credit cards for personal expenses.

Not keeping these two very different financial activities separate will cause you to have problems with your accounts, with your record keeping, and with your taxes. Keeping these activities separate will be an easy process that will save you lots of headaches.

Conclusion

You'll find that, so long as you make your own decision and are comfortable with it, you'll feel in control. The decision to pay off your debts is a very adult decision, and the process that must take place in order for that to be accomplished requires planning, discipline, motivation, and confidence—all adult qualities.

The decision to file bankruptcy is also a very adult decision and requires a good deal of examination of all your options. If you make the decision based on what is best for you, and if you have confidence in yourself, then any decisions you make, no matter how difficult they might be, will sit well with you.

Let us reiterate this about credit: Although few people living in our society seem to realize this, credit is the process by which we obligate ourselves financially. Please make your choices with awareness. Your financial well-being depends on it.

CHAPTER NINE

Bankruptcy

What is bankruptcy? How does it work? Is it an option you should consider? If you are reading this chapter with more than idle curiosity, you're probably concerned about your debts. You may be receiving letters or calls from collection agencies, or it may be that you are seeing all too much of your paycheck absorbed by debt payments every month. Or you may have been hit with a horrendous and unexpected debt, such as for a hospitalization, which you see no possibility of ever repaying.

This chapter will take away the mystery surrounding bankruptcy, and will present it for what it is—a legal and reasonable option for people who are overwhelmed by their debts and need a fresh start in their financial life.

When reading this chapter, please keep in mind that every individual's situation is unique. Each person has a different financial situation as well as emotional makeup. Some people's debts are to their family members, employers or partners, so there are strong social forces against their going bankrupt. For some people, no decision is more personal than the decision of whether to go bankrupt. Therefore, there are no rules—just good information, and good decision-making.

You will learn a lot of factual information in this chapter. There are two types of bankruptcy for consumers, which are discussed in the section headed "Chapter 7 and Chapter 13 Bankruptcies." A section entitled "Which debts are discharged in Chapter 7 bankruptcy" contains information about discharge (elimination) of debts. A section on exempt property under Chapter 7 discusses what property a debtor can keep in a Chapter 7 Bankruptcy.

Since all people considering bankruptcy are concerned about the effect bankruptcy will have on their credit and financial standing, as well as the emotional and social implications, we include a section on the effects of bankruptcy.

With these facts, plus all the other information about your financial situation, which you have discovered in the course of developing your plan, you will read the section "Is bankruptcy right for you?" to evaluate your particular situation to make the right decision.

Finally, we have included some "Tips for Going Bankrupt" which will make the process a little easier if you decide bankruptcy is the right decision for you.

Terminology

Some terminology used in bankruptcy is pretty technical and not used in the ordinary sense. The most important of these terms are as follows:

Assets. A person's "assets" are things (land, money, furniture, stocks, anything else) that she owns.

Debtor / creditor. If you owe someone money, you are that person's "debtor," and that person is your "creditor." (Many of us are both debtors and creditors, because we will owe money to, say, the bank, but someone else, like our brother, will owe us money.) If you go bankrupt, you are the debtor, and everyone you owe money to is a creditor.

Debts / liabilities. These two words mean the same thing. The money that a person owes to someone else is a debt or liability.

Discharge. A discharge is a technical term in bankruptcy. It means the elimination of debts. Debts that are discharged in bankruptcy actually cease to exist. The purpose of a discharge is to give the debtor a fresh start with fewer or no debts.

Exempt Property. The term exempt property is also a technical term. Exempt property is property that a bankrupt person does not have to give up in a Chapter 7 bankruptcy. This will be explained more thoroughly below in the section exempt property under Chapter 7.

Secured Debt. A secured debt is a debt where the debtor has given or pledged something to the creditor to secure the loan. Whatever is pledged is called collateral. Collateral can be anything of value. For example, your car is collateral for your car loan; (remember, the bank holds the title to the car until you pay off the car loan). If the debtor does not pay the loan, the creditor can take the collateral, sell it, and apply the proceeds of sale against the loan amount. Some of the more common secured debts are a home loan secured by a mortgage and a car loan secured by the car.

Surrender. A bankrupt person in a Chapter 7 bankruptcy may be required to surrender (give up to the trustee) property that is not exempt. The trustee will then sell the property and divide the proceeds of sale among the creditors.

Trustee. A bankruptcy trustee is an official of the bankruptcy court who handles the property and debts of a person who has filed bankruptcy. A trustee is usually a lawyer, and often is the only bankruptcy court official with whom the bankrupt person will come in contact. The trustee's duties are described below, in the section on Chapter 7 and Chapter 13 Bankruptcies.

What is Bankruptcy?

Bankruptcy is a legal proceeding under the Bankruptcy Code. The Bankruptcy Code is a federal law, enacted by the Congress of the United States, under the authority of the United States Constitution, which regulates proceedings in situations where people or companies cannot pay all of their debts. People with overwhelming debts may use bankruptcy to gain control of their financial situation.

People whose debts are greater than their assets, or who cannot pay their debts as they come due, are permitted to "claim bankruptcy" (go bankrupt). They do so by hiring an attorney, who will prepare and file a petition in a federal bankruptcy court. The petition lists all of the assets and all of the debts of the person going bankrupt. A notice of the bankruptcy filing is sent to every creditor of the person filing the petition.

As soon as the creditors receive the notice of the filing of the bankruptcy petition, they are prohibited from contacting the bankrupt person in any way. They cannot call or write any letters, pursue any lawsuit, repossess any property, or do anything else to collect the debt they are owed. For people whose creditors have been harassing them, this is a wonderful relief.

Usually, the bankrupt person needs to attend one legal proceeding, called a first meeting of creditors. At this meeting, creditors are entitled to ask the bankrupt person questions about her financial situation. However, many times no creditors come to the hearings.

If everything is in order in the bankruptcy, the debtor is allowed the relief requested in the petition. Depending on whether the bankruptcy is a Chapter 7 bankruptcy or a Chapter 13 bankruptcy (see next section for a discussion of the differences between these two types of bankruptcy), the debtor may receive a discharge of some or all of her debts (Chapter 7), or a payment plan may be instituted under which the debtor pays the debts off gradually (Chapter 13).

Chapter 7 and Chapter 13 Bankruptcies

The terms Chapter 7 and Chapter 13 refer to two different chapters in the Bankruptcy Code.

Chapter 7 and Chapter 13 bankruptcies are very different in their results. Chapter 7 is a liquidation type of proceeding, meaning that the debtor's property is sold to pay debts. Chapter 13 is a reorganization type of proceeding, and in fact, Chapter 13 is often not even thought of as a bankruptcy.

Under Chapter 7, many or all of the bankrupt person's debts are discharged. On the other hand, the debtor is required to surrender all of her property except for exempt property (see Exempt Property Under Chapter 7, below).

Under Chapter 13, debts are not discharged, and the bankrupt person does not have to surrender her assets. Instead, the bankrupt person's debts are reorganized. A payment plan is worked out under which the bankrupt person pays a set amount out of every paycheck to the bankruptcy trustee, who then divides the payment among the creditors. The payment is based on the amount the bankrupt person earns in income at the time the bankruptcy petition is filed.

Chapter 13 is a very desirable type of bankruptcy if a person has non-exempt assets that she does not want to part with, or if she has debts that cannot be discharged in bankruptcy.

Which Debts Are Discharged in Chapter 7 Bankruptcy?

All debts can be discharged in a Chapter 7 bankruptcy except for those specified in the Bankruptcy Code as not being dischargeable. The most common non-dischargeable debts are tax debts (federal, state, and local), and student loans made or insured by a governmental body (unless the bankrupt person has been making payments on them for five years or more).

A person who has substantial tax debts or student loan debts may find that Chapter 13 works better for her. In fact, Chapter 13 can be very attractive as a way to pay off such debts. Interest stops accruing on the debts, the payments are affordable to the bankrupt person, and the IRS or the student loan collectors cannot seize the bankrupt person's assets.

In the case of a student loan, the bankrupt person can make payments under Chapter 13 until she has been repaying the loan for five years. She may then convert the Chapter 13 into a Chapter 7 and have the remainder of the student loan discharged under that chapter.

For all practical purposes, a tax debt can never be discharged and must be paid in full, but the payments under Chapter 13 can be made comfortable.

Even a person who selects Chapter 7 may choose to continue making payments on certain debts. Such debts are usually secured debts. If you have a debt that is secured by your home, your car, or some other property, and do not want to make the payments on it any more, you must give up the item that secures the debt. In other words, if you want to get rid of your house payments, you must give up your house. If you want to get rid of your car payments, you must give up your car. Most people who go bankrupt want to keep their car, their house, and their furniture. If this is their choice, then after the bankruptcy they will still have to continue these payments. On the other hand, some people choose to give up some of these assets so that they may also give up the debts.

Exempt Property Under Chapter 7

Remember, the basic principle of Chapter 7 is that you give all of your assets to the trustee, and all of your debts are discharged. However, you may claim certain property as exempt. There is no one rule as to what property is exempt, because exemptions vary from state to state. You will have to ask your attorney what property is exempt in your state. Just as an example of what might be exempt, there is a federal statute, which your state might have adopted, that exempts $7,500 in equity in a residence and certain other property such as $1,200 in value of a car, or $4,000 worth of household furniture. On the other hand, some states will exempt the entire value of a homestead (the house you own and live in), even if it is worth $1,000,000, but only a few hundred dollars worth of other property.

Does this mean you might have to give up the valuable antique ring that Aunt Agatha bequeathed you? It might or might not—you'll have to ask your lawyer. Often a trustee will not bother with non-exempt items adding up to only $1,000 or so, because of the trouble in selling them.

If you have some item or items of property that you are not willing to part with as part of a bankruptcy, you might consider Chapter 13. Your debts are not eliminated, but the debt payments will be something you can handle, and you will probably be allowed to keep your assets.

Effects of Bankruptcy

People who are contemplating bankruptcy are concerned about the effect it will have on their credit and on their personal and professional relationships. Does going bankrupt necessarily ruin your credit for years to come? Will people make fun of you or think less of you because you go bankrupt? Can your employer fire you for going bankrupt?

It will probably surprise you to learn that bankruptcy will not necessarily ruin your credit rating. Whether it does depends on your credit rating before you went bankrupt, what types of debts you had when you went bankrupt, and the other circumstances of your bankruptcy.

The most common single cause of bankruptcy is large hospital bills for an uninsured illness. If you have always had good credit, but are considering bankruptcy because of such an unexpected event, and the only debts you have are your medical bills, your bankruptcy will probably not affect your credit. At the most, a potential creditor might ask you to explain your bankruptcy or to furnish a copy of your bankruptcy petition. The same rule holds true for a bankruptcy triggered by some other unusual event not involving ordinary consumer debt.

On the other hand, your credit rating will be adversely affected by your bankruptcy if your credit record is already poor because of delinquent debt payments. A bad credit rating is not the end of the world. You don't need credit unless you intend to borrow money. You may need some breathing room—a period of time during which you don't use credit and, instead, manage your money on a cash basis.

An alternative to handling your finances on a cash basis is to begin dealing with credit card companies that specialize in offering credit to people who have gone bankrupt. Why would a creditor want to do this? The reason is simple. If you have gone bankrupt in a Chapter 7 proceeding, you cannot go bankrupt again in a Chapter 7 proceeding for six years. These lenders then have six years to (1) encourage you to incur new debts, (2) charge you exorbitant rates of interest, and (3) use the most aggressive collection techniques available to obtain their money. Please avoid these creditors. They can make your life miserable.

It is very pleasant to live without any debt. A person can have a perfectly good life without having good credit. You simply pay cash, and save money for the bigger items.

What about the social implications of going bankrupt? This is what makes the decision of whether to go bankrupt such a personal matter. We all care about the good opinion of others, even of people who really are not important in our lives. And it is a fact that some people will sneer at someone who goes bankrupt. These people are making a mistake, though. Everyone, male and female, rich and poor, experiences difficult times in the course of their lives. The difficulties may not necessarily be financial, but they will be difficulties nonetheless. It is the height of folly to sneer at others during times of stress, knowing it is inevitable that our stressful times will come also.

One of our clients was a lawyer who went bankrupt. Because the bankruptcy hearings of many debtors are held in the same afternoon, and all of the debtors have lawyers, a number of lawyers were present at her bankruptcy hearing. They started snickering when she stated she was a lawyer. She then described the circumstances of her bankruptcy. She had been a partner in a large law firm. The law firm had suddenly collapsed. She and all of the other partners were left with several million dollars of debt. She had no other debts. The lawyers listening to her testimony became quieter and quieter. Their faces were very grim by the time she had finished her testimony. It was apparent that they were thinking about their own law firms and wondering whether the same thing could happen to them. And they were right to wonder—because it could. As we said in the introduction, none of us are ever absolutely in control, or absolutely secure, or absolutely powerful. We all just do the best we can do in any set of circumstances.

Rather than feeling defeated by the social implications of bankruptcy, ask yourself whether it would be beneficial or detrimental to you to do the things you would have to do in order to pay your debts. Ask yourself! Bankruptcy is a legal, financial decision. It should not be made from a place of pride, or a place of self-destruction, or a place of approval-seeking. Your decision should be made with your best interest at heart. Would not going bankrupt mean you would have to take a second job? Would it mean you would have to move to a different city? Would it require that you sell your house or other property? In short, would you have to totally change your way of life?

Doing the things you would have to do to pay your debts may appear to you to be a welcome challenge. If so, feel confident that you have made the right decision. On the other hand, if arranging to pay these debts seems to require that you kill your reasons for living, bankruptcy might be a better choice. Either choice is a good choice, so long as it is made with awareness and with your own best interest at heart.

We have never counseled a person choosing to go bankrupt who was not delighted with her choice. On the other hand, our clients who have accepted the challenge of paying off mountainous debts have felt much stronger for the experience. In dealing with debts, as in so many other areas, the power of choice, and deliberately choosing in one's own best interest, seem to be the keys to personal satisfaction.

Is Bankruptcy Right For You?

Before deciding whether bankruptcy is the best choice for you, be sure to explore all other options. In order to make the best choice, you must know what the choices are.

You are already doing one good thing in reading this book. Pay special attention to Chapter 8 on credit. It will show you how to work your way out of a credit crunch. The other chapters will show you how to control your income and expenditures so that the optimum amount of money is available to pay your debts.

Consider the possibility of developing a plan to pay your creditors out of whatever portion of income you have available to pay debts. It may not be necessary to pay the minimum charges or to pay the debts off in full. Many times, if you have a serious plan that covers all of your debts, and if you communicate clearly with all of your creditors and stick to your plan, they will accept what you are trying to do.

Seek financial counseling, if there is someone in your area who offers such a service. A counselor may identify a choice you have overlooked.

Most importantly, choose to do what is best for you. We guarantee, you will be happy with your choice.

Tips for Going Bankrupt

You can't just read this or any book and decide to go bankrupt. You need more information about your specific situation. This is one occasion in your life when a good lawyer is a necessity. Only after discussing your situation with a lawyer and finding out the exact result of your bankruptcy can you make a good decision.

If you decide to consult a lawyer about bankruptcy, you have a lot of work to do. First, you must select one. The best way is to ask a friend who has recently had a divorce or filed for bankruptcy which lawyer she used and whether she was satisfied with her choice. You could also call the state bar association (the state association for lawyers is usually called something like the "California Bar Association" and is usually located in the state's capital city), and ask whether there is a specialization for bankruptcy lawyers in your state. You could then get a referral from the bar association. Many lawyers also advertise in the yellow pages and in newspapers, and there is nothing wrong with selecting a lawyer from an advertisement. However, be prepared not to hire the lawyer if you do not have a very good feeling about her or him.

When you go to see the lawyer, don't hire the lawyer unless you feel comfortable with him/her. The lawyer should see you in person, should return all your phone calls promptly, and should be respectful and diligent. Bankruptcy documents should be prepared within a week or two after you supply all the information requested.

The lawyer will probably require payment in advance for filing the petition. A typical fee for an uncomplicated Chapter 7 or 13 is in the range of $500 to $900, depending on where you live. In addition, there is a court filing fee of $120. Your lawyer can advise you about suspending payments on your bills in order to save money to go bankrupt.

You will need to supply your lawyer with information about all of your debts and assets. If you omit any debts or assets from your bankruptcy petition, the bankruptcy judge may deny your bankruptcy. All questions on your petition must be answered truthfully.

Do not try to beat the system by shuffling around or concealing your assets. It is highly unlikely that you will think of some technique that has not been used in the past. The consequences for concealing assets are severe—at the least, your bankruptcy may not be granted. If you prepay certain favored creditors before you file, they may be required to pay back the amounts you paid them. In addition, if you buy luxury items or take cash advances shortly before filing for bankruptcy, those debts may not be discharged. Your lawyer can advise you about legal ways to plan your bankruptcy to your best advantage.

Conclusion

Bankruptcy is a legal option for the relief of intolerable debt. In and of itself, it is not good or bad; it is neutral. It offers one more choice for the resolution of financial difficulties. It may or may not be the right choice for you. But don't deny yourself the power of considering this choice while you're considering other choices.

The preceding chapters have addressed hard dollars-and-cents issues and the related emotional issues of self-esteem, control and power. The following chapters address primarily emotional issues—compulsions and addictions, relationships with partners, and your feelings—and their related financial components.

Compulsions and Addictions

What are compulsions and addictions, and what do they have to do with personal money management? As we said in the Introduction, there are many psychological obstacles to good money management. From the time we began counseling clients, we noticed that some of our clients did the same things over and over again which impaired their ability to manage their money wisely. It was obvious to us from the first that compulsions and addictions could and often did interfere with good money management.

What are compulsions and addictions? In this chapter, we will define compulsions and addictions, and name some of the most common affecting good money management. We will show *how these compulsions and addictions can hamper or even* *destroy a good money-management plan.* Why do we have compulsions and addictions? We will share our clients' stories and ask you to look at addictions and compulsions in a different way. Finally, we will give you some tips on seeking help for addictions and compulsions.

What Are Compulsions and Addictions?

A compulsion is an irresistible impulse to perform an irrational act. For example, some people have the irresistible impulse to always pick up the check when they are eating out with others. If you are eating with such a person and try to pay your fair share, you will become overwhelmingly aware from the intensity of his or her response that this is a very emotionally-charged situation. One look in her eyes will tell you that you're not having a discussion about money.

We have all known someone whose house has to be absolutely perfect at any cost. Such a person may put every penny into its renovation and maintenance, having little or nothing left for groceries or entertainment. Some people will constantly go to school, acquiring one advanced degree after another, without ever feeling ready to actually begin a career. Workaholism is a compulsive need to work beyond what is expected or compensated.

The need to incur the seeking-approval expense, which we mentioned earlier, is also a compulsion—the compulsion to please or impress others in order to get their approval. An example of this type of expense is spending thousands of dollars you don't have to landscape the yard so the neighbors will think well of you. Financially, this means making decisions with little concern for your financial well-being. Some of our clients have beggared or bankrupted themselves to put on a good show for their bosses or boyfriends—who possibly would not have appreciated the show, had they known the cost.

All of the compulsions mentioned above involve spending excessive amounts of money. Another, equally unbalanced compulsion is the compulsion to save (the "tightwad syndrome"). People with this compulsion may arrange *never* to pick up the tab, and may even abscond with part of the tip. They may unnecessary deprive themselves of decent food, convenient transportation, and suitable clothing. They may also deprive their children.

What are addictions? Addictions are a type of compulsion. They involve the uncontrollable need to ingest a substance or perform an activity which directly alters mood. For example, alcohol is an addictive substance, as is heroin. These substances directly alter mood. Food also alters mood, and some people become addicted to food.

Activities which are well-known to alter mood include gambling, religion, sex, spending, and incurring frightening amounts of debt. Of course, a person can engage in these activities without being addicted, but when a person *must* engage in a mood-altering activity, losing free choice, that person has an addiction.

Compulsions and Addictions Can Hamper or Even Destroy a Good Money-Management Plan

Some addictions and compulsions have such a direct effect on a person's ability to stick with a money-management plan that they must be dealt with if the plan is to succeed.

Expensive Addictions. Some addictions are just simply too expensive for a person with an ordinary income. Someone with a drug habit that costs $500 a week and a salary of $300 a week won't be able to make a money-management plan work. Of course, that's an exaggerated example. But even an addiction to cigarettes can make a significant dent in a small income, and various other addictions can be too expensive to be consistent with good money management.

Compulsions to Spend Money. Some people have a compulsion to buy things; other people have a compulsion to get deeply in debt. Another compulsion that directly involves the spending of money is gambling. Still another is a compulsion to give large sums of money away (for example, to television evangelists). If you have a compulsion to spend uncontrollably, to get deeply in debt, to gamble uncontrollably, or to give away unreasonable sums of money, your plan cannot possibly work until you have the compulsion under control.

Addictions That Impair the Ability to Think. By their very nature, compulsions are irrational; however, only some of them directly impair the ability to think. For example, we saw many clients who were addicted to nicotine, but the addiction didn't prevent them from going to work, earning a living, and making good money-management decisions. However, a serious addiction to alcohol or to certain other drugs may prevent a person from being able to function in their job and to develop a financial plan. No one can actually implement the details of a financial plan while intoxicated.

Addictions or Compulsions with Which a Money-Management Plan Interferes. Don't kid yourself: if your money-management plan is going to interfere with an addiction or compulsion, one or the other of them is going to have to go. Chances are, it will be the money-management plan. If you could make your plan work, except that you have been in the habit of spending $100 a month on alcohol, and you intend not to spend the money any more, but you have not really decided to stop drinking—well, the result is pretty obvious. You will desire to drink, you will decide to drink, you will buy alcohol, you will decide your plan doesn't work, and you will be right back where you started. Don't defeat yourself from the beginning. You can accommodate a drinking habit by allocating a certain amount of money each month to alcohol. Or you can decide to stop drinking. But you can't expect a money-management plan that directly interferes with an exist-ing compulsion or addiction to succeed.

Why Do We Have Compulsions and Addictions?

There are many theories about why people have addictions and compulsions. Our clients tell us, and it is our personal ex-perience, that the feelings that seem to be alleviated by compul-sive behavior are very unpleasant. Some of our clients who experienced great anxiety readily admitted that they had learned to alleviate that anxiety with compulsive or addictive behavior.

For example, we had a client who was a workaholic. She worked long hours without adequate compensation. She felt pretty well while she was working, but always experienced anxiety attacks, insomnia, headaches, and other very unpleasant symptoms if she was forced to take a day off. The only way she knew to alleviate these symptoms was either by going back to work (which her family disapproved of) or by drugging herself by drinking alcohol and smoking. The method she used didn't matter—the important thing to her was to make sure those bad feelings didn't get to the surface.

Knowing the unpleasantness of living with a high degree of anxiety, we found it very easy to understand why some of our clients engaged in compulsive behavior, since the compulsive behavior reduced or eliminated the anxiety for at least a short while.

From the experiences we have had with our clients and from the stories they have shared with us, our (nonexpert) impression is that people may have compulsions and addictions for three reasons: because life is often hard, because we all have feelings, and because we are very adaptive creatures.

Compulsions and addictions seem frequently to be adaptive responses to tough situations. They seem to be used to help people cope with unpleasant emotions. Some of the most unpleasant emotions our clients demonstrated, as you might imagine, were the fear and guilt associated with not handling their money well. We watched many of our clients make financial decisions clearly not in their best financial interest, and carry these decisions out, all in an attempt to reduce the unpleasant feelings of having money problems to begin with. The results were, of course, sometimes disastrous.

One of our clients, feeling frustrated and somewhat depressed by her inability to control her debts and to manage her money, went straight to the local department store and promptly spent about $2000 trying to lower her anxiety level, raise her spirits, and somehow, in a weird way, control her money. The pleasant feelings which this shopping spree induced were short-lived, and the debts seemed everlasting.

We did not criticize these clients. We did not criticize their decisions. We learned to see our clients' use of compulsions to suppress their unpleasant feelings and to continue functioning as an illustration of their hardiness and their ability to survive, rather than as traits for which they should feel guilty or ashamed, or chastise themselves. We encouraged them to acknowledge these strong survival qualities and perhaps to redirect this energy into improving the quality of their decisions for the future.

Not all of our clients' addictions and compulsions seemed to be connected to stressful current situations. We had one client who had a serious problem with spending money excessively when she went out of town. It turned out that when she was a child, the family trips were nightmares. They were always trips to visit relatives, and her parents spent the entire trip telling the relatives what a horrible child she was. When she became an adult and took a trip, she compulsively spent in order not to feel the low self-esteem she associated with going out of town.

Another client was born into an immigrant family who had fled Europe during World War II. All of their relatives left behind perished during the war. In addition, all of the family's valuables were stolen as soon as they arrived in the United States. Although the family had worked and managed to live comfortably in America, and in fact our client had never experienced deprivation of any kind, the intergenerational feelings of deprivation were very strong. Our client's anxiety was alleviated only by *not* spending money. She lived frugally, to say the least. Her standard of living was far below what she could have afforded.

If we all were treated with love and respect at all times in our lives, we might see far fewer addictions and compulsions. However, life just isn't like that. No matter how fortunate we have been in our lives, we have all suffered some trauma. Some of us have suffered severe trauma. Some of us are presently in situations that bring us a great deal of sorrow and hardship. If we do not perceive any alternatives to the current difficulties in our lives, it is very understandable that we resort to some types of behavior which offer us even a small respite from anxiety.

While it's probably better to live without compulsions or addictions than with them, we don't counsel our clients that they need to be compulsive about getting rid of them. Our clients do not come to us because of their compulsions or addictions. They come to us because they want to learn to manage their money better. If the presence of a compulsion or addiction arises that thoroughly sabotages the money-management plan, we take the opportunity to look our client straight in the eye and to present their choices to them.

Seeking Help

In our country at the present time, there is a great deal of attention being focused on addictions and compulsions. Many experts have written books on various aspects of this type of behavior. Your local bookstore probably has a special section on this topic, and your library may occasionally feature books on addictions and compulsions. Self-help groups, the best-known of which is the "twelve-step program" of Alcoholics Anonymous, have increased in numbers to a phenomenal degree. There are twelve-step programs for people addicted to narcotics, sex, debting, gambling, and many other addictive substances and activities. (There is some controversy, however, over whether the traditional twelve-step programs are appropriate for some women because they emphasize humbling oneself rather than developing strong self-esteem. Non-traditional programs are available in some cities.)

Many counsellors and physicians now have a great deal of expertise in this area. Because some compulsions and addictions apparently have a physical, as well as an emotional component, some physicians may recommend the use of drugs to reduce patients' problems with compulsions and addictions.

We can't recommend one course of action over another; our clients who have dealt with compulsions and addictions have sought help from a variety of sources, and have often reported success after trying several different approaches or a combination of approaches.

The cost of treatment is always a concern to our clients. Treatment for compulsions and addictions can range from being free or inexpensive to costing a great deal of money.

The least expensive assistance is free twelve-step programs. To find these, look in your newspaper (often in the personal ads) or the yellow pages of your telephone directory.

The next least expensive assistance would be from books, either from your library or bookstore.

If you decide to seek therapy with a counsellor, there may be a mental health center in your community that provides counselling at fees which are commensurate with your income. If you wish to obtain therapy from a counsellor in private practice, but the cost is a concern to you, first check out the possibility of group therapy. This is almost always less expensive than individual therapy. Also be very direct with your therapist about money. Tell her or him about your financial situation and see if you can reach an agreement about payment that will fit into your financial plan.

If you are covered by health insurance, be sure to check your policy to see what the coverage is for therapy. Some policies provide limited or no coverage, while other policies provide very generous coverage. Some policies only cover therapists with certain qualifications, and you will need to seek a therapist with those particular qualifications to obtain coverage.

Don't take the word of the employer's benefits manager as to what is covered. We have often had clients who were told that their therapy was not covered when it actually was. In fact, don't even take the word of your health insurance booklet. The booklets sometimes say that certain treatments are not covered, when state law requires insurance companies to cover the treatment. For example, some states have laws requiring insurance to cover equally treatment rendered by psychologists and psychiatrists; yet the insurance booklets might state that only treatment by psychiatrists is covered. If you are told that the treatment you want is not covered, you might want to check with a lawyer who is knowledgeable about health insurance.

Don't give up! Our clients who decided to obtain treatment for their addictions and compulsions tried various approaches, but they all had one thing in common—they didn't give up, at least not permanently. If they saw no result from one course of action, they went on to another.

Conclusion

If you choose to deal with a compulsion or addiction as part of developing a personal money-management plan, you will have doubled the beneficial results of developing your plan. If you decide not to deal with a compulsion or addiction, you have still exercised your power of choice. Don't berate yourself for your choice; congratulate yourself for knowing yourself, knowing what you can tolerate, and going ahead to do something positive for yourself by implementing your money-management plan.

Never lose sight of the overall point of this book. Money is only one element of your total financial picture. Each time you attempt to make a money decision, an array of factors comes into play that may seem to have nothing to do with dollars and cents. Compulsions and addictions are part of the emotional side of money management. We encourage you to acknowledge this side and to give it the credence it deserves.

CHAPTER ELEVEN

You and Your Partner (or There's No Such Thing as a Free Lunch)

Personal money management when you are single and living alone is relatively simple. You may have your own emotional issues about money, but at least the issues and the money are yours. The scenario is not more complicated than that.

Once your finances become entangled with someone else's, though, you inevitably become involved in what we call "relationship money management." The technical details of money management can still be simple, but the emotional elements can complicate the situation. In this chapter, we will describe several techniques for successful relationship money management.

Since many people are in a financial partnership other than a marriage, we use the term "domestic partnership" to describe various types of financial partnerships, including marriage. We begin by answering the question, what is a domestic partnership? The process of establishing a successful money-management relationship begins with assessing your financial arrangement and its evolution. We will show you how to do this.

Having discovered some possible trouble spots in the current arrangement, you will be guided in ways of changing that arrangement. These guidelines will be directed at achieving fairness, equality, and control. To achieve fairness, we will determine the value of services, as well as monetary income. We will describe various models for fair and equal financial partnership arrangements, depending on different domestic and financial situations.

We will advocate a woman's control of her own finances and make specific recommendations about which arrangements are most effective. Then we will show you how to implement the plan. Finally, we will tackle the non-financial aspects of a financial partnership—the emotional issues (including the emotional issues of power and control) and the reality that—because of death, divorce, and other changes—*relationships don't last forever.*

Following the suggestions of this chapter may illuminate the strengths of your personal relationship. You and your partner may be able to manage your finances together with respect, equality, fairness and a good balance of control. If that is the case, you and your partner will appreciate each other even more after reading this chapter.

On the other hand, you may find that following the suggestions of this chapter will cause you, your partner, or both of you, a great deal of stress. Don't abandon the idea of good money management—and don't abandon your partner just because you are experiencing some stress or frustration. Stress in this type of situation—where you are trying to do something good for your-self—is an indication of a special opportunity to examine your-self, your partner, and your relationship, to set aside some of the myths of your relationship, and to become more firmly balanced in reality.

Our hope that, if you take good care of yourself financially, you may also take good care of yourself in other areas of your life is never stronger than with regard to your important relationships. We hope that fairness, equality, and a good balance of control achieved in the financial area will translate into other areas, and strengthen your personal relationships in every way.

The Domestic Partnership

For our purposes in this book, we are defining a "domestic partnership" as any primary, committed, relationship between two adults that is intended to be long-lasting, regardless of its legal status or society's view of it. The domestic partnership, and to some degree all personal relationships, have an economic com-ponent.

The economic factor in one type of domestic partnership, the marriage, is obvious. There are many laws that define the financial rights and responsibilities of spouses to one another. Husbands and wives can be required to contribute to the support of one another; and with few exceptions, they cannot totally disinherit one another; divorce is at least as financial as it is emotional.

There are no laws governing the financial relationship of domestic partners who are not married except for the law of contract—courts will usually enforce any agreement which the partners have made. Domestic partners who are not married need to pay particular attention to their agreements, committing all of them to writing, a major point detailed on page 204.

The primary financial feature of a domestic partnership is that the partners' finances are intertwined to some degree. Because there is just one household, and two people, both are involved in the economics of running the household. In most cases, both partners contribute money to the household. Both partners also contribute services to the household. Sometimes, one partner contributes all of the money, and the other partner all of the services. If you are a partner in a domestic partnership, think about what you and your partner each contribute to the partnership in money and in services.

Become more aware of your system of relationship money management. Ask yourself the following questions:

- How much do I make in income? How much does my partner make?
- How much does it cost to run our household?
- How much money do I require as an individual? How much does my partner require?
- Do we each have individual savings accounts, or do we have joint savings?
- Do we each have retirement plans? Are they for a similar amount, or are they for different amounts?
- How do we contribute our incomes to the household?
  1. Do we use a joint checking account into which all our money is placed;
  2. Do we contribute only those portions of our income necessary to pay the household expenses; or
  3. Do we contribute every time an expense occurs?
- Do we contribute the same amount of money or amounts based on our incomes? Do I pay certain expenses while my partner pays other expenses? Or does one of us pay all the expenses?
- How do we divide services that contribute to the household? Does one of us do most or all of the

household work, or do we divide it, equally or unequally?

- Does either of us feel they are working too hard, either at a place of employment, at home, or at a combination of the two?
- Does either of us ever complain of unfairness in the way work at home or money is allocated?
- Who manages the household money? Are decisions shared, or does one person make all decisions? Does one person write all the checks to pay bills, or is this responsibility shared?
- Does one partner have sole control of the checkbook?
- If your partner manages all the household money, have you ever felt that your household money would be better managed if you managed it or if you participated in the management; do you think you are a better money manager than your partner?

When you are asking yourself these questions, don't pass judgment. Just be aware that there are many different ways of managing a financial partnership, and that the way you and your partner manage your partnership is just one of those ways.

Also, be aware of how your system of relationship money management developed. The two of you may never have discussed exactly how to manage your money, and you may not have deliberately decided to manage your household one way rather than another; you may have just fallen into a pattern when you started living together, without consciously making a choice. Many partners fall into whatever pattern they learned from their parents, even if that's not the best system for them.

Now is the time to be aware that you are your own person, your partner is their own person, and your partnership is unique. Once again, make a choice with conscious awareness and in your own best interest; choose the management system that works best for you, as well as for the partnership.

Joint and Separate Expenditures

In order to discuss financial management in the context of relationship money management, we must introduce the concept of "joint expenditures." These are household expenditures, either fixed or controllable, which are for the benefit of the entire household and not just for one person. Examples are most fixed expenses, such as rent or mortgage and utilities, and controllable expenses such as food, house maintenance, and expenses of minor dependent children.

Examples of fixed and controllable expenditures that usually are not considered to be joint expenditures are payments on a student loan; clothing and personal grooming expenditures; hobby expenses; lunches with friends; and even large expenses such as a piano, car or computer that are really bought for the benefit of one partner.

Because it is not always clear which category certain expenses fall into, each couple must discuss and decide which of their expenses they consider to be joint, and which they consider to be separate.

What Is Fair in Relationship Money Management?

As we said at the beginning, fairness is one of the big issues in relationship money management for women who are in domestic partnerships. If a financial arrangement between two people is fair, it will enhance their relationship and their respect for one another. If the financial arrangement is inherently unfair, it will breed bitterness, resentment and disrespect.

The myths that pervade our society can cause women to have a great deal of difficulty perceiving what is fair and what is not. There are several reasons for this difficulty.

First, as we will discuss below, women tend to undervalue the services they perform that do not result in monetary compensation. Second, most women are raised with the myth that they should extend themselves, give without reckoning, and generally make free contributions without asking for anything in return. Women are pressured by everyone—their families, churches, government, and society—to give too much. Generously giving of time and money is one of the joys of life, but women are encouraged to do this to their own detriment. It is possible to balance taking care of yourself with giving of yourself.

Third, the old myth that "good girls are taken care of," clouds women's vision until it is difficult to see at all. Being a good girl means doing whatever anyone wants without asking for anything in return. Thus, the good girl myth redoubles the general message of giving without seeking something in return. Although the myth seems to offer the return that the "good girl" will be entirely taken care of, it's apparent that's not true.

One look around, however, confirms that that myth is only a myth, one that leads many women to degradation and despair. Women live in poverty, together with their children, in far greater numbers than men do. In fact, women who head single-adult households live in poverty almost three times as frequently as men who head single-adult households, and more than six times as frequently as households headed by two adults.*

Women continue the important societal work of rearing children under the most adverse circumstances. After giving so

---

* U.S. Department of Commerce Publication: *Poverty in the United States, 1988-1989.*

much, they are abandoned by the people to whom and the society to which they have contributed. The plain fact is that society has been taking a free ride on the backs of women for several thousand years.

In our own personal financial relationships, we can put aside the myths, open our eyes, and seek true fairness. Fairness can be found in a relationship where our partner fully values our contributions and supports our desire and need for independence and personal choice.

The first step to ensuring fairness is documentation. Whatever your financial arrangement may be, get it in writing, signed by both you and your partner. Run it past an objective third party to get an outside opinion. A signed document would not be so important if women were treated fairly and equally in our society. Because that is not the case, get the agreement in writing.

If you have any property other than your personal effects and household goods, it would be a good idea to have a lawyer review the document. The attorney can make sure the document is unambiguous and can advise you whether it needs to be witnessed or notarized. If you decide to employ a lawyer, find out in advance how much the services will cost.

Married couples can also enter into written agreements, although state laws concerning marriage can sometimes interfere with the full legal enforcement of such agreements. (Unmarried couples may actually have more freedom to contract than married.) We counseled one wife who together with her husband wished to divide up the marital assets. The husband was changing careers and wanted assurance that, in the event of their divorce, he would have sufficient funds to complete the training for his new career. Several years later, they are still married. (Such an agreement may not be enforceable in every state; but the parties in this example were willing to accept some legal uncertainty.) If an agreement of this sort is important to you, obtain good legal advice as to its enforceability.

It is not unusual for couples to enter into written agreements. We advise many unmarried couples who wish to have their partnership arrangements properly documented. For example, each of the partners in one lesbian couple we counseled owned a house. They lived in one house and rented the other to a tenant. They wanted to put the title to both houses in joint names with right of survivorship (so that if one partner died, the other would own the house automatically). But they also wanted to insure that if they separated, each of them would get her own house back. This was simple enough to accomplish using written documents. But don't attempt such a serious transaction without the assistance of a skilled lawyer.

If you are in a non-traditional relationship, especially a lesbian relationship, you may be concerned about how to locate a lawyer who has the appropriate expertise, will take your legal needs seriously, and will treat you and your partner with respect. In many cities, there are lesbian and gay switchboards listed in the phone book that can give a caller the names of lawyers who wish to work with lesbian clients.

What is Equality?

We have used the word "equality" several times, and in the introductory section indicated that it was not necessarily "sameness." During the 1970s, women thought they knew what "equality" meant—they thought it meant the same opportunities and the same pay that men had. By the 1980s, many women were about to drop dead under the weight of "equal opportunity." In addition to their former full-time job of maintaining a household, rearing children, and caring for aged and ill relatives, they now had the equal chance to hold another high-pressure, full-time job in the marketplace.

So what is equality? The best definition we could come up with is that equality exists when elements that are the same are treated the same, and when elements that are different are treated differently, but in a fair way. For example, if one partner is caring for an incapacitated grandmother, and the other is not, they are not in the same situation. It would be unfair for them to contribute equally to the household in outside work and housework. Women must be able to have equality without sameness, or we will not have equality at all. And ultimately, equality is closer to fairness than to sameness.

What is Fairness?

While you might feel that a financial arrangement perceived by both partners to be fair is fair, that is not always the case. Feelings of guilt, fear, or duress can and will inhibit partners from freely perceiving fairness accurately. Fear can cause a partner to grasp more than is objectively fair, or to give up their share entirely. Duress by one partner can force the other to make decisions they would not otherwise make.

If both partners judge an arrangement to be fair, freely and without fear, guilt, or duress, that arrangement will be fair for them.

If it is impossible to reach a financial arrangement that satisfies both partners, that's usually a sign there is an emotional factor that needs to be dealt with. See "Emotional Elements in Relationship Money Management," below.

Whatever type of financial arrangement you and your partner have, ask yourselves two very important questions: (1) Are you both satisfied with the arrangement? and (2) Do you feel comfortable with the division of money?

It is hard to define true fairness, but once the emotional elements are removed, you will know it when you see it.

Value of Services

As we said above, partners contribute two things to a domestic partnership: money and services. Avoid the common practice in our economy of undervaluing or assigning no value to services that are not directly compensated by money. Because of this practice, women's contributions, many of which are not monetarily compensated, have been almost totally ignored in the economy.

For example, if your teen-age son works for McDonald's frying hamburgers, this service is given a particular value of four or five dollars an hour. He brings the money home and is a "breadwinner." However, if his mother cooks exactly the same hamburgers at home, no labor is recognized, and no value is placed on it. The family (and, all too often, the woman herself) will be at a loss as to how to value that service or whether to value it at all.

Similarly, the woman who cares for her aging father is simply a good daughter. Her services are valueless. They do not compare with $30,000 or more a year that the same services at a nursing home would cost.

One serious result of the undervaluation of services at home is that it allows women to work outside of the home as though that were their only job. Because neither these women nor any other member of their families count the job at home as "work," it is very common for Dad and the kids to watch Mom work eighteen to twenty hours a day without a second thought.

Work at home *is* work, and has the same value as any other work. Don't let anyone tell you otherwise! And lots of people will try to. If you work outside of the home, and also work a full job at home, you are working two full-time jobs. You and everyone else may be calling it something different, but that's what it is. Keep this in mind when you start thinking about developing a relationship money-management plan with your partner.

Paradoxically, the services of women and men in the home have been valued much more in the past than they are in most households today. The farmer husband and wife contributed equally, both in the field and in the home. No matter how the actual chores were divided, it was abundantly clear to both partners that their joint efforts were critical to their survival.

Services were actually valued more when they, rather than cash money, kept the family fed, clothed and sheltered.

If you or your partner had to hire someone to cook, clean, or tutor your children, these services would cost substantial amounts of money. Just because cash does not actually change hands does not mean these services are worth less. Just because you do these services, rather than someone else, does not mean they are value-less. Think about all you and your partner contribute in services to your household, and assign monetary or other countable values to these contributions.

Because defining fairness in general is impossible, let's look at some sample arrangements that provide a framework of fairness in a variety of possible situations.

Assessing Each Partner's Contributions to the Joint Finances

Equal Contributions of Services and Money. It is reasonable for two working people who have similar salaries to contribute equal amounts of money to the joint household account. It is also reasonable for them to share household obligations equally. All personal expenses and most, if not all, savings are separate (see "Control Your Own Finances," on page 210).

Similar But Not Equal Incomes. If each partner earns a full-time income, and the incomes are not substantially different, it is appropriate for them to share household expenses proportionately to their incomes. For example, if one person takes home $1,000 per month and the other person takes home $2,000 per month, the one with the higher income pays two-thirds of the rent, utilities, etc.

Food and similar joint controllable expenses may be divided fifty-fifty or may be divided proportionately. In either case, each partner takes care of their own personal expenses and savings out of their own income. Contributions of services are shared equally, because both partners are working full-time jobs outside the home. Some partnerships we counseled have found this method a relief from more traditional methods.

When the Income Disparity is Great. If the disparity is very great (for example, if both partners work full-time, and one takes home $5,000 a month and the other takes home $1,000 a month), there are two possible approaches: First, the couple may divide household expenses proportionately; or second, the partners may combine the two incomes and reallocate the total for the equal benefit of both partners. (In our example, the total income of $6,000 would be divided between the partners, either fifty-fifty or by some other fair, mutually agreed-upon formula; and the household expenses would then be divided equally between the partners.) Services are contributed equally, as each partner is working full-time.

One Partner Contributes Money and One Contributes Services. One partner provides the primary income. The other has no income, or works part-time for a small income, and provides services to the household. The money from the primary income is shared between the partners. The joint expenses and all fixed expenses are paid out of the primary paycheck, and the remainder of the paycheck is divided between the partners, either fifty-fifty or according to some other formula that the partners consider to be fair. One couple we counseled allocated a somewhat larger portion of the paycheck to the partner who worked outside the home because of that partner's greater need for lunches, clothes, and personal grooming expenses.

One Partner Provides All the Money While the Other Develops a Career, and is Similarly Accommodated in the Future. You are taking a chance deferring your plans until your partner is through school, or gets a new business off the ground, if you expect to have your partner accommodate you in the future. Thousands of women have been burned by trustingly agreeing to work while their husbands went to medical school or otherwise developed their careers. All too often the husbands have found someone more compatible during the last years of medical school or residency, and the wives have received a divorce with no support. This is not fair.

If you enter into this type of arrangement, *get it in writing.* Be very specific as to what you will do to support your partner, and what your partner will do when your partner's turn comes to support you. This arrangement is fair only if the future promises are fulfilled. Guard your own right to fairness by having written proof of your agreement with your partner. A written agreement of support between either married partners or unmarried partners should be enforceable under normal contract law, through a legal proceeding if necessary.

Control Your Own Finances

Why manage your own finances? There are two primary reasons why every woman would want to manage her own finances. First, managing one's own money is one of the things that adults do. Children are taken care of, but grownups take care of themselves. Managing your own money is a crucial way of taking care of yourself. This doesn't mean you shouldn't ask for advice. It is always wise to consult with someone more knowledgeable than yourself. But don't surrender your power of choice and your power of control.

The second reason a woman should manage her own finances, and participate in joint decisions with her partner, is that women need to make sure their money is well taken care of. Many women who are perfectly good money managers want to believe their partners are particularly competent in that area, and surrender all control to them. Later (especially if the relationship doesn't work out, or the partner dies, leaving little or nothing), they realize that they would have been better off if they had been more involved in making financial decisions.

There is nothing about being male that gives a person an edge on money management. The men we have seen did not have good money-management skills when they came to us, and they, along with all of the women, were able to develop their skills in this area. After all, what names first come to mind as experts on money management? Sylvia Porter for one. Jane Bryant Quinn for another. But regardless of whether men are better money managers than women, or women better than men, the fact is that every adult person should take responsibility for their own finances.

Arrangements for Managing the Joint Finances

The Wrong Ways

The partners in a typical modern couple deposit all of their incomes into a single joint checking account. They consider all of the money "our money." Out of this checking account, they pay their fixed expenses and their joint controllable expenses. The balance typically disappears in miscellaneous purchases. Deposits into savings (also joint) are sporadic. Neither partner really takes responsibility for making the most out of the family income. The end result is that "our money" becomes "no money."

An alternative scenario is where one partner takes over the family finances entirely, and the other partner must ask for money for even the smallest purchase. It is still not uncommon for a husband to totally manage the family finances, leaving the wife completely in the dark and completely dependent.

We have even seen more than one case like this where the wife was a professional who worked full-time and had a large income. In that case, the wife was able to write checks on the joint account, but the husband controlled her spending of money through intimidation.

In both of these scenarios, the parties have misapplied the elements of responsibility and control. In the first instance, neither partner was really taking responsibility. In the second instance, one partner had surrendered all control. None of the people in these examples are really exercising their full adult powers to be responsible financially.

We have never seen two partners lump all their money together into a single joint account and end up happy with the results. That doesn't mean it can't be done; but we have never seen it happen.

The Recommended Arrangements

There are two basic arrangements that we recommend. The first is to keep everything totally separate, and the second is to have a joint account for joint expenses, but individual accounts for individual expenses and savings.

There has always been, and to some degree there still is, pressure to combine finances totally once you enter into a relationship. This is just as true for same-sex relationships as for hetrosexual relationships. This is not only not necessary, but in many cases it is ill-advised. Don't run your finances the way your parents ran theirs, or the way your friends run theirs, unless those particular methods suit you best also. Manage your finances in the way that is most advantageous to you. If either partner feels at all uncomfortable about combining money, the money should be managed separately by each partner. Many partners prefer to keep all finances totally separate. They have their own checking and savings accounts, and, when a joint expense arises, they each write a check for their share.

The second arrangement we recommend is to have a joint checking account for joint household expenses and individual checking and savings accounts for each partner. That way, each partner may exercise the adult privilege and responsibility of deciding what to do with their money.

How does this work? The partners set up five accounts: one joint checking account, two individual checking accounts, and two individual savings accounts. All of the accounts can be joint accounts with right of survivorship (so that the surviving partner will automatically become the owner in the event of the death of the other partner), but each partner will control one checking and one savings account.

The partners agree as to how much money each is going to contribute into the joint checking account. This money will be used to pay all joint expenses. If the joint expenses in any month turn out to be more than the amount contributed, the partners will contribute additional money according to their pre-arranged agreement.

The partners then deposit the remainder of their incomes into their own accounts to save or spend according to their own personal money plans.

These are the two basic arrangements we recommend, but, depending on the goals of the partners, many variations would be suitable, provided they are based on fairness. For example, both partners may wish to contribute to a joint savings account for a down payment on a house, or a college fund for the children.

Implementing Your Plan

The steps we have discussed for you to take in order to begin controlling your own money are as follows:

- You and your partner write and sign an agreement that you both believe to be fair.
- You set up the savings and checking accounts necessary to carry out your agreement.
- If you have a paycheck, deposit it into your own checking account, and write checks according to your partnership agreement and your personal money plan.
- If your partner's income is the primary one, be sure you are paid your share of that income and then implement steps one through three.

Joint Credit / Joint Tax Returns

If your domestic partnership is a marriage, you may choose whether to be personally obligated on your husband's tax debts and other debts. We recommend that, with the exception of the mortgage, you choose not to be obligated for your husband's debts. Generally, you are not legally obligated for your husband's debts unless you have signed a document agreeing to be responsible. There are a few exceptions to this rule; for example, in some states you could be responsible for the necessities of a dependent husband. However, if your husband goes out and spends $2,000 on camera equipment, he hasn't put *you* in debt unless he charges the purchase to a credit card or account that you have agreed in writing to be responsible for.

If you sign a joint tax return where money is owed, you owe the money the same as your husband. We had one client whose husband was self-employed. He failed to pay his quarterly tax returns, and she signed a joint return where the tax due was in the five figures. Several years later the tax was still unpaid and she was seeking a divorce (for other reasons). She was more worried about this debt than any other aspect of her financial situation. If any taxes are due on a joint return because your partner failed to make appropriate tax payments, file your tax return separately rather than jointly.

Similarly, any credit cards, charge cards, loans, or other debt that has your name on it is 100 percent yours, just as it is 100 percent your husband's. If enough loan payments are not made in a timely manner, your personal credit report will be just as bad as your husband's. You should review very closely any credit that has your name on it.

If you want to separate your debt from your partner's as part of your implementation of your plan, take your name off all these accounts. If you have any doubt at all about your partner's reliability with regard to credit, or if he complains about your review of the accounts, it is particularly important to have your name removed. All it will take is a phone call and a letter. Don't delay. You will still owe the money already charged or loaned at the time you have your name removed, but your husband cannot incur additional debt against your name on those accounts.

You can always open your own accounts, for which you will be solely responsible.

If you have concerns related to taxes or debt, add numbers five and six to our implementation list:

- You remove your name from joint charge cards, credit cards and lines of credit.
- You set up your own charge cards, credit cards, and other accounts.

Emotional Elements in Relationship Money Management

We have heard all our lives that if a couple is arguing about sex, their real issue is money, and if they are arguing about money, their real issue is sex. Whether this is actually true or not, it illustrates a basic reality: If you and your partner are arguing about money, the real issue may not be money at all.

In fact, we will set down a rule here that we believe to be true: It is impossible to be emotional about money. Money is entirely neutral, and can do no harm. If you are arguing about money, and one or both of you feels any anger, sadness or fear, the argument is not about money. It may be about control. It may be about deprivation. It may be about insecurity. It may be about anger. It may be about abuse. But it is not about money.

Can You Argue Without Getting Mad, Sad or Scared?

Yes, sure you can. That's not to say you won't get excited, hammer on the table, stand up to make a point, and otherwise get very animated. After all, this is an argument we're talking about. But in your gut you may not feel angry, sad or scared.

What if one of you does feel angry, sad or scared? The most important thing to do is to realize that you are no longer arguing about money. Terminate the argument immediately, and instead, explore where those feelings are coming from. They may be a reaction to something the other partner just did or said in the course of the argument. Or they may be a reaction to something that happened in the past. If it happened in the distant past, the person feeling emotional may not even be aware of what happened to give them those feelings. But *something did happen,* whether they know it or not.

The important thing to do is to acknowledge the feelings and deal with them before going back to the money discussion. If your partner is the one feeling emotional, re-establishing their trust in you might be necessary before proceeding. Assure your partner that you are not trying to take advantage, be unfair, or ignore their feelings. If you are feeling emotional, tell your partner as much as you can about how you are feeling. Ask your partner to support you and help you. If you are both feeling emotional, or if one or both of you feel confused, you need to cool off by yourselves or consult with someone outside of the relationship. Don't proceed with the money discussion until both of you are free of other baggage, free to keep the discussion about money. In other words, wait until you are grounded in the present.

Abusive Relationships

Many of us are in abusive relationships. Many of us are unaware that our relationships are abusive. There is almost always a financial element to an abusive relationship.

An abusive relationship exists if one partner tries to control the other through manipulation, confusion, or intimidation. The classic abusive relationship is the relationship of the physically abusive husband and the battered wife. He intimidates her by threatening physical harm. She believes him because he has beaten her in the past. Through intimidation, he can control her.

Another fairly straightforward type of abuse occurs when a partner shouts insults at the other partner. To prevent the abuser from shouting, the abused partner allows herself to be controlled.

A more subtle type of abuse occurs when a "breadwinner" husband refuses to allow his wife access to any money. He may control her by promising to give her money if she does what he wants.

A frequent technique of an abuser is to try to confuse the abused person. The abuser may deny the evidence of their victim's own senses and accuse them of being crazy, or the abuser may lie about their actions or motives until the victim is unable to sort fact from fiction.

Because the goal of an abusive relationship is for one partner to control the other, and because most people equate money with control, an abusive partner will almost always be abusive about money. They will make no attempt to be fair, but will instead try to get most of the family's resources. They may literally control the checkbook and deny their partner access to funds. They may manipulate the partner into purchasing things the partner doesn't really want.

If you are the victim in an abusive relationship, your partner's need to control will be threatened by your attempts to change the way in which you manage your money. Don't be surprised by displays of anger and other controlling behavior. As long as your life is not threatened, you can go ahead and implement your money plan. There is the remote possibility that your firmness in taking control may actually make your partner feel more secure, reduce their need to control you, and possibly reduce the abuse.

If you suspect that you are the abuser, you're already ahead of the game. Abusive people rarely recognize that their behavior is inappropriate. Having this insight is the first step toward changing your inappropriate behavior. This will give you a unique opportunity to improve your relationships with your partner and with yourself. However, be aware of this: The need to control, which is behind all abusive behavior, comes from fear. You will have to be vigilant to protect and comfort that part of you that feels fearful.

Changing an abusive relationship is a very challenging task, and a good counselor or therapist can be an invaluable ally. You and your partner might put obtaining the services of a first-rate therapist at the top of your list of financial priorities.

In addition, there are many books on abusive relationships. Check at your library or bookstore. Whether you are the abuser or not, abuse is a very serious problem, and we urge you to seek all the support you can.

Relationships Don't Last Forever

Many fairy tales end with the words "and they lived happily ever after." As little girls, we probably heard those words thousands of times. How could they fail to leave a lasting impression?

The plain fact is, though, that *all* relationships come to an end. Some end quickly and acrimoniously; some end by mutual agreement; some end after decades, with a gentle death. But they all end. We believe that women who choose to be in a relationship should make provision for the end of that relationship as early as possible.

Many people have the superstition that, if they make a will, they will die earlier, or that, if they make a partnership agreement with their domestic partner, which governs the division of property in the event of separation, the relationship will come to a screeching halt. These are very dangerous superstitions because they keep people from taking care of their partners and themselves.

Execute a written agreement as to what will happen to your property if the partnership is terminated, wills that provide for the disposition of property upon the death of one of you, and powers of attorney, which provide for the management of property if a partner becomes incapacitated. Budget enough in your money plan for a lawyer to prepare appropriate documents.

These documents are very important for married couples; they are even more important for partners who are not married. Because marriage is a legally sanctioned relationship, state laws act as wills for married people, specifying that the spouse will get a certain portion of the estate upon death, and providing for the division of property upon divorce.

However, partners who are not married will not be able to inherit anything upon the death of the other partner, and, without a written agreement, it is anyone's guess how a court would divide the partners' property if one of them sues the other following a separation.

Having a written partnership agreement is also imperative in two other situations. The first such situation occurs when one partner agrees to defer or give up a career in order to accommodate the other, with the clear understanding that, in return, the other partner will support them for a period of time or for the rest of their life. Because women experience pay inequity at every level, it is very common for a wife to be in the position of giving up her job in favor of her husband's higher-paying job. Without a written agreement, courts award very inadequate alimony to divorcing spouses and nothing to unmarried partners.

The second situation occurs when the partners agree to something like this: "I'll support you through medical school, and then you'll support me while I get my Ph.D. in psychology." If this relationship ends before the entire bargain is fulfilled, and if the partners do not have a written agreement stating their arrangement, it is unlikely that a court will require either partner to fulfill their end of the bargain.

Conclusion

While we have made every effort in this chapter to stress equality in relationships, we are not oblivious to the fact that women have traditionally and historically been disadvantaged. We are all too frequently bombarded with the news of women being victimized by their partners economically, emotionally, and physically. This book is mainly about money management; but it has been our wish from the beginning that women who seek to control their finances will seek to control other areas of their lives as well.

If you are being victimized by your partner, put a stop to it. Do whatever you have to do to make good choices for yourself. Don't worry about the past or the future. The past is gone, and you won't have much of a future if you don't do what you need to do in the present.

Congratulate yourself and take the first step!

CHAPTER TWELVE

You and Your Feelings

Throughout this book, we have stressed the importance of being aware of your feelings. Financial plans ordinarily succeed unless there are strong feelings working against them. This last chapter, which deals explicitly with both feeling good and feeling bad, begins with a description of how to pay attention to your feelings.

Next, we deal with the importance of honoring the validity of those feelings. There is always a reason that you have the feelings you do. Honor those feelings, and the life experiences you have, which give rise to them.

We then describe the "feeling good" part of good money management. These are not feelings to strive for, but feelings that will naturally arise if you are successful in your money-management plan. We tell you not to be afraid of feeling too good or of being too successful, fears that have limited women's achievements for centuries.

The next section will deal with the "feeling bad" part, which can often prevent you from carrying out a money-management plan.

Finally, we spend some time debunking myths that traditionally have kept women from achieving in many areas, including business and finance. We focus on the reality that women are capable of managing their own lives and their own money, that they can seek to do whatever is in their hearts, and that they are entitled to recognition for their accomplishments.

Pay Attention to Your Feelings

Every human being experiences many feelings every day. There are hundreds of words in the English language describing feelings in their many colors and shades, including happy, joyful, powerful, confident; and angry, sad, terrified, confused, impotent, or ashamed. In and of themselves, feelings are neither good nor bad. We tend to think that only the positive feelings such as happiness, confidence, and so forth, are "good" feelings. But it is also good, or at least appropriate, productive or constructive, to feel ashamed if you lie to your partner, or to feel sad if someone you love dies, or to feel terrified if you hear a prowler in the house.

The important consideration is not whether or not you have certain feelings (because you *do* have many different feelings), but how aware of them you allow yourself to be. The more aware you are of your feelings, the better they can help you learn from what's happening in your life right now, as well as from what has happened to you in the past.

This chapter deals most explicitly with emotional issues as they relate to money management, and as they relate to a person's conscious control of various aspects of her life, including money.

Ask yourself frequently, "How am I feeling?" One reason to ask "How am I feeling?" is to see how the answer relates to your overall behavior, including money behavior. If you're not already in the habit of doing this, you may feel very strange at first, and may also have some difficulty in identifying how you feel. But your ability to know how you're feeling will improve with practice.

It may help a great deal to talk with someone else about how you're feeling. It can be practically impossible to figure out what's going on inside of you by yourself. A trusted friend or partner, or a good therapist or counselor, can help you with this process by asking you questions that let you explore your feelings, thereby holding up a mirror to allow you to see yourself more clearly.

Your greatest opportunities to help yourself in this process will come when you are having very strong emotions. If you find yourself uncontrollably and unreasonably angry with your partner or child, for example, that is a real opportunity for you to figure out what's going on inside you. Perhaps you have stored up anger from completely unrelated incidents. Try to welcome these episodes, as painful as they are. They are opportunities to gain healthier perspectives.

We want to share one example of how being aware of your feelings can have a direct impact on a financial plan. One of our clients who otherwise was successful in managing her finances spent an unusually high amount of money on groceries and dry goods. She was totally unaware of the discrepancy. When invited to her house, we were astonished to see the incredible inventory of products stockpiled in cupboards and on shelves. Over dinner that evening, she related a story to us, without any awareness of how revealing this story was. Her father had lost his job when she was ten years old. The family had been forced to sell off its possessions in order to move to another town, and, for a long while, the family finances were extremely tenuous, to say the least.

When we suggested that there might be a relationship between this past event and her present spending habits, she experienced the same feelings of sadness, fear and anger that she had felt as a child. As an adult, these same unpleasant feelings haunted her. Stockpiling goods was a technique she used to suppress her feelings. Being aware of these feelings allowed her to identify and see more clearly that particular childhood event, which had produced the feelings, and to ground herself in the present, where her living situation was not in jeopardy. Therefore, she found that the excessive buying was not necessary, and was able to eliminate this barrier to success in her plan.

Honor the Validity of Your Feelings

Your feelings are correct, whatever they are. They're based on some reality, either past or present. Honor their validity at all times.

This doesn't mean that you must act on your feelings. You can always choose whether or not to act; all of us have feelings every day that we choose not to act on.

However, your feelings are good information, to be taken into account along with other information available to you. If you feel distrustful of a salesperson, pay attention to that feeling. They may be trying to swindle you. Your feeling may prompt you to investigate their character. If you feel confused whenever you talk to your boss about a raise, your boss may be manipulating you. If your partner says "you're crazy" every time you express your opinion, your feelings of anger and frustration are obviously well-founded.

Why not act on every feeling? First, all of us have impulses or feelings every day that, if followed, would have us performing actions ranging from inappropriate to possibly illegal. You may want to kill your boss, for example, but such an action would surely cost you your job, at the very least.

Second, feelings do not always relate to present situations. If you're in a situation that reminds your subconscious of some traumatic event that happened in the past, you may have a feeling that is totally appropriate to what happened in the past, but not appropriate to what is happening in the present. That was the case with the client who stockpiled goods. There was no reason in the present for her to feel insecure, but her subconscious connected an excess of goods with security to such an extent that it influenced her actions in the present.

If you have a powerful emotion, try to evaluate whether it is too strong for the present situation. That will be a good guide as to whether it relates to some past event more than to what's going on in the present.

Feeling Good (and Feeling Bad about Feeling Good)

We hope you are discovering as you work through this book, there are plenty of good feelings that come with developing and implementing a money-management plan. It's very important to be aware of these good feelings and to enjoy them. Let's validate some of these feelings right now.

You are experiencing enhanced self-confidence. You have accomplished something new and important. You have proven your competence. You can do anything you want to do.

You also feel greater self-esteem. You are a valuable person, and you have shown your belief in your own importance by taking very good care of yourself financially.

Feel powerful. You are. You have exercised your personal power in your own best interest. You have overcome obstacles with great courage. You are strong.

Because of your own knowledge, you can evaluate whether you can rely on someone else. You can judge whether they are capable and will act in your best interest. You know whom to trust and whom not to. You can confidently enjoy the feeling of trusting someone who is trustworthy.

We stress again—do enjoy these feelings! Most women are taught from the earliest ages not to succeed, not to be capable. You may be going against your early childhood training, not only in feeling competent and powerful, but in enjoying those feelings. You may feel some guilt at having these strong, positive feelings. You may have a sense of foreboding, that something terrible will happen.

In our society, we frequently connect success in women with adverse consequences. Psychologists who tested medical students by asking them to complete a story, which started with "Alice" making the top grades in her medical school class, found that many students, both male and female, completed the story by having Alice run over by a truck, shunned by her fellow students, or otherwise experiencing negative consequences. Testing a different set of students with the same story, but with the main character named "John," produced endings where John was attracting women and reaching great success.*

So, as you can see, a strong feeling of foreboding may be cultural and not related specifically to you.

Give any negative feelings you might have as much credence as any others. Explore where they come from. Is there something in the present that is causing these feelings? We have certainly known of many instances where a woman's partner was not supportive of her or appreciative of her success. We counseled

---

* Martina S. Horner. "Sex Differences in Achievement Motivation and Performance in Competitive and Noncompetetive Situations." Ph.D. Dissertation, University of Michigan, 1968. University Microfilms #6912135 (cited in Gilligan, Carol, *In a Different Voice* [pp. 14-15], Harvard University Press, 1982).

one successful professional woman whose husband supported her career in words, but criticized her for not spending enough time doing housework. The more successful she was, the more critical he became. He was obviously giving her a double message about her success. While supposedly supporting it, he was actually imposing a serious adverse consequence on her in the form of his criticism.

For many of us, there are no adverse consequences in the present, and our negative feelings are purely the product of childhood and cultural messages. Regardless of the source, you may need as much courage to appreciate yourself for your good work as it took to implement your money plan in the first place. Give yourself credit for this courage as well!

Feeling Bad

Negative feelings can sabotage a good money-management plan faster than anything else. In fact, they are the primary factors that can ruin a money-management plan. You might think that some unexpected large expense (large vet bill; new air conditioner) would be the most likely event to ruin a plan. But the truth is, any plan will take the unexpected into account or will work around it after it occurs—unless negative emotions crop up, telling us, "the plan will never work *now*".

Although feelings are not masculine or feminine, we were all reared in cultures and in a society that taught us ways women are supposed to feel and be. We can't help having this training influence our lives. But the more conscious of these culturally taught feelings we are, the more able we are to work around them or to get rid of them. Let's explore some of these feelings.

Fear of Making a Wrong Decision

Many women are afraid to do certain things because they're afraid of making a wrong decision. They are afraid to buy stock, for example, because if the stock value declines, it will be proof that they made a mistake. The truth is, no one can predict the future. No one can predict whether a stock value will go up or down. Yet millions of shares of stock are traded every day. The only decisions that can be characterized as "wrong" are those that are made without obtaining good information and without thinking about the decision. If you do these things, your decision is as good as it can be.

Many of us have friends or relatives who seem to just sit around waiting for us to make a "wrong" decision so they can criticize us.With that type of "support," how can we ever feel self-confident? How can we ever make any decision? Just remember, your friends and relatives may not really have your own best interest at heart. They are very likely to have a strong interest in maintaining the status quo. For example, if you are all poor, they might not feel comfortable if you improved your financial situation. If they're uneducated, they could feel that you would no longer be "one of them" if you were to obtain an education. They may not want you to move out of town to pursue a career.

We had one client who wanted a college education. Her parents, who were not college-educated, were very much against it. Finally, they grudgingly realized that they could not stop her, but they made it as hard on her as they could. She could go to college, but only if she supported herself totally, paid all of her college expenses, paid them rent, did all of the housework, and mowed the lawn once a week. When she graduated from college and announced she was moving out of town to pursue her career, they were far more upset about how their lives would be changed by her absence than pleased for her success.

If your friends or relatives are not supportive, just keep in mind that they are not on your side. That will help you clarify what is going on with you and with them. You may need to find some new friends who will be more supportive.

Partners can be the best or the worst. They can be your biggest ally, helping you to feel good about yourself and what you are doing. We had one friend who worked and went to law school. She married while in her second year of law school. Her husband was extremely supportive in word and deed. Not only was he obviously proud of her, praising her at every opportunity, but he also did all of the cooking, all of the housework, and generally took care of her personal needs.

On the other hand, if a partner is critical and unhelpful, you may feel that doing something for yourself is all too much trouble. In either case, acknowledge the situation fully, and discuss it with your partner. If your partner is not supportive and will not discuss the issue or agree to be more supportive, you definitely will have some emotional barriers to overcome. We again suggest that you find a friend or counselor who will provide the emotional support you need.

Feelings of Helplessness or Futility

Many women are actually taught to be helpless, so it's no wonder that these feelings persist. Many women are, in reality, helpless, in the sense that they're not taught ordinary living skills, such as managing money, or making household repairs. Of course, skills can always be learned, so "real" helplessness need only be temporary. The emotional feeling of helplessness may be a little more difficult to deal with.

Remember, that feeling is there for a reason. Many women believe they'll be taken care of if they're helpless. Moreover, their own belief that they can't take care of themselves provides a strong motive, a survival motive, for appearing to be helpless.

If you experience feelings of helplessness, remember where they come from. If you wish to overcome them and be self-suffi-cient and strong, you may do so. However, you may need first to teach yourself that you can take care of yourself. You should pursue everything you can think of will give you this message, whether it's getting a degree or certificate, learning self-defense, or developing a money-management plan. Good luck!

Feelings of futility, such as "why bother," or "it doesn't matter anyhow," may be a realistic reaction to an existing situation, or may be a symptom of depression. During the Cold War, many people took the attitude that nothing mattered very much, because we were all going to be blown up by the atom bomb anyway. Later events have indicated that it is more realistic to act as if we have a future. Many women have very realistically felt that it did no good to save money, because their husbands would take it away.

Depression

People suffering from depression may lose their ability to manage their money. We had one client who had always handled her money without any setbacks. Then, over a two-year period she experienced an inordinate amount of change and loss in her life. The deaths of several people close to her finally took their toll. She became depressed, unable to function as she always had, and unable to keep control of her money. When she finally emerged from this difficult time she found her finances in shambles and began the challenging task of reorganizing and managing her funds once again. Even the best money-management skills can fail you if you suffer from depression.

Feelings of Guilt

Most of us were taught to feel guilty early and often, and these feelings can persist and influence our lives every day. Guilt is part of our religious and cultural heritage, and far more of it is heaped on women than men. You may feel guilty if you spend too much on your son's shoes, or you may feel guilty if you don't buy him the shoes he wants. You may feel guilty if you save money, or you may feel guilty if you don't save money. The truth is that there is practically nothing you can do or not do that you can't feel guilty about.

Feelings of guilt can adversely influence your money-management plan. It can simply be too painful to proceed with the plan. Or you may feel guilty about trying to do anything positive for yourself.

Guilt can be very difficult to deal with. It frequently is accompanied by feelings of unworthiness, that is, feelings that you are not entitled to anything. Rather than dealing directly with the guilt, attack the feelings of unworthiness by proceeding to do good things for yourself. You may have to start with very small things. But keep demonstrating to yourself that you are worthy and entitled to what you want.

A warning: doing this may bring many very sad feelings to the surface, because treating yourself well may remind you of the many times in your life when you were not treated as a person of value. However, we can all survive sadness and feel better for having honored the feelings. Don't let it stop you from doing something positive for yourself.

Your feelings of guilt should gradually slip away as you take better and better care of yourself.

Fear of Confrontation

Generally speaking, men learn the art of confrontation from their cradles. Studies have shown that boys spend a great deal of time in any game arguing about the rules. Girls tend to avoid confrontation, canceling the game if there is a disagreement. We are taught to avoid confrontation, to smooth things over, even if it means giving up our position.

If you have a partner, the two of you will inevitably disagree from time to time about how to spend money or how much money to save. If you're willing to disagree with your partner, strongly stating your point of view, you will feel powerful, even if you ultimately decide to agree with your partner.

On the other hand, if you give in every time they state an objection, you'll feel weak and disregarded. You'll be treating yourself with disrespect. You may even become angry with your partner. For many reasons, it's far better to be willing to engage in confrontations with your partner than to give in every time there is a disagreement.

If you decide to begin engaging in confrontations for the first time, tell your partner what you're going to do, and ask for support while you learn how to argue. You may want to select something to argue about that is not very important. You'll be a little scared at first. You may become unreasonably angry. You may feel silly or stupid. But if you continue, you will feel empowered, and you will come to enjoy your disagreements. There is no reason why they should not be fun.

Just remember a few things. Stick to the point. Don't change the topic of the argument, no matter how much you're tempted to do so. If you both become angry, stop arguing until you cool off (it's all right for one of you to be angry at a time). Terminate the argument if either of you becomes abusive in the slightest. Don't get stuck on a position. Stay flexible. The ideal result of an argument is a resolution that satisfies both partners. Let yourself have fun. You should both feel good, not bad, about the argument.

Reaction to Abuse

Abuse keeps us from feeling good about ourselves, so it is important to identify abusive behavior. Many of us are abused by our partners. Often, we are very unhappy with our primary relationship, but unless our partner is beating us, we don't recognize that we're being abused. The following statements are abusive and are made to control and manipulate. If you hear your partner saying one of these, your partner is abusing you.

"You're crazy." This is a classic. Women have frequently, through the centuries, been incarcerated by their partners on the pretext that they were crazy. It is the ultimate put-down, stripping you of all dignity and personhood. When you set out to implement your money-management plan, your partner may tell you that you're crazy. They will also tell you that we're crazy. You're not crazy. Your partner is abusive.

"You're not feminine." You are a woman, therefore feminine. Being feminine does not mean being helpless and stupid. It means being strong, capable and courageous. We have protected our children and provided for them, as well as for ourselves, from the beginning of time. Be strong in your femininity, as women have always been.

"You're a lesbian." Well, you may be a lesbian, in which case you'll say "what's your point?" But if you're not a lesbian, this remark is intended to insult and control you. Tell your partner he's a lesbian. It makes as much sense.

"You're just not good with money." Maybe you are, maybe you're not. If you're not, you're trying to become good with money. That's what this book is all about. There is not a "money gene" we either have or don't have. You can learn to be good with money, and you intend to do so. This is just another put-down.

Any attempt to confuse you. Confusion is a sign that you are being abused. If you feel confused after talking to your partner, chances are they're trying to manipulate you. A person who is acting in a loving manner will be clear and truthful with you.

What if your partner does abuse you? You have several choices. First, you don't have to do anything about it. You can be completely aware but leave things as they are.

Second, if you want to change the abusive behavior, don't absorb it. Throw it back in your partner's face. If they call you a name, call them a name. If they're intimidating you physically, you can either return the intimidation, or separate yourself physically. If they confuse you, refuse to listen.

But let's face it. Living with an abusive partner is unpleasant at best and dangerous at worst. We are opposed to the abuse of women. Ask yourself Ann Landers' famous question, "Are you better off with them, or without them?" If you decide that you're better off with them, then we urge you to seek counseling to help end the abusive behavior.

Debunking More Myths

In *How to Suppress Women's Writing*, Joanna Russ brilliantly exposes the methods by which women's artistic endeavors have been discounted and ignored through the last several centuries. We believe the same techniques she describes for the suppression of women's writing apply to other efforts by women as well. Paraphrasing her outline and applying it to money management, we perceive that society has suppressed women's achievements, now and during the past several centuries, by means of the following reactions:

"She can't do it." Historically (in the not-too-distant past), society has denied her access to jobs, banks, financial advice, refused to teach her to read or do arithmetic, and kept her ignorant, poor, and out of touch. In addition, there were laws prohibiting her from owning her own property. Now women are discouraged, rather than legally barred, from attempting achievement.

"She didn't do it." Her husband, father, financial adviser, or accountant did it.

"She did it, but she shouldn't have." She makes herself ridiculous and unfeminine. She'll never get married if she's so independent.

"She did it, but it wasn't worth doing." All she did was manage the household money so efficiently that they could live

on one income instead of two and give their children the benefit of a fulltime mother. Or: all she did was work as a nurse while taking care of a household and children.

"She's the wife of a doctor, lawyer, etc." Don't even talk about what she did. Just assign her the role of wife and ignore her accomplishments.

"She did it, but she only did the one thing." She only made a fortune in the stock market, not in real estate. She only started and built a cookie company, not a steel mill. She's good at managing the household finances, but she wouldn't be any good at running a business.

"She did it, but no other woman could have done it." Ignore the fact that women have been running households, farms and businesses, alone and with partners, since before recorded history. It's easy to do, because women are rarely granted any recognition. Let every woman feel that she is the only one who ever attempted anything. Most of all, deprive women of female role models by denying recognition to women who would be good role models.

"She did it, but she's more than a woman." She has a strong "masculine side" which really accomplished the good money management. Her "feminine side" was of little use to her, as usual.

Let's set these myths aside. Let's say, "We did it. It was worth doing. We could have done anything else we wanted to do. Other women have done the same thing. It's not special in the sense of being anomalous, but it is very, very good."

Conclusion

You may have many emotions while carrying out your money-management plan, some positive, some negative. There are strong social and cultural messages working against independence for women, which can produce feelings of guilt or inadequacy if they are not recognized for what they are. An abusive partner can cause a woman to feel confused, or to feel that her efforts are futile.

On the other hand, good money management can make you feel competent and powerful. These feelings will be your greatest encouragement as you work your way *From Paycheck to Power*.

Glossary

- **401-K** A retirement savings plan offered by an employer where the employee's contributions are tax-sheltered; usually a percentage is matched by the employer.

- **Acceleration Income** All income that is not Baseline Monthly Income. It can be used to accelerate your plan.

- **Addiction** Uncontrollable need to ingest a substance or to perform an activity for the purpose of altering mood.

- **AFDC** Aid to Families with Dependent Children. A welfare program.

- **Alimony** Payments made by an ex-spouse under a divorce decree.

- **Assets** Everything you own.

- **Bankruptcy** A legal means of eliminating or controlling the payment of your debts.

- **Baseline Monthly Income** Money you regularly receive as income each and every month.

- *Charge Card* Card issued by a merchant or retailer, extending credit for use only at that store or company.

- *Compulsions* Irresistible impulse to perform an irrational act.

- *Controllable Expenses* All expenses that are not Fixed Expenses, and over which you have a great deal of control.

- *Credit Card* A card issued by a bank or credit company, which you can use in various places. Visa and MasterCard are examples.

- *Credit Union* A savings and borrowing institution, similar to a bank, which only members can use. Large employers often sponsor credit unions.

- *Credit* The legal arrangement by which you incur debt.

- *Debt* Money you owe.

- *Federal Income Tax Withholding* Money taken out of your paycheck for federal income taxes. Your paycheck stub will show this withholding.

- *FICA* The deduction from your paycheck for Social Security. It shows on your paycheck stub.

- *Fixed Expenses* Living expenses payable every month over which you have very little control because the amounts are set by someone or something else. For example: mortgage/rent, utilities, car payment.

- *Gross Amount* With regard to a paycheck, the total amount, without any deductions such as taxes. (Compare: Net Amount)

- *IRA (Individual Retirement Account)* Investment for retirement in special account which has certain tax benefits.

- *Net Amount* With regard to a paycheck, the amount you are left with after all deductions are taken out. (Compare: Gross Amount)

- *Roll-over* The process of transferring retirement funds from one account to another. The term is also used when money in one investment (such as a CD) is transferred to another investment (such as another CD).

- *SEP (Simplified Employee Pension) Plan* Investment plan for retirement in which contribution is deducted from employee's income.

- *"Seeking Approval" Expense* Expense incurred to obtain the approval of someone else and not out of a sense of necessity or desire.

- *Specific Item Loans* A loan you take out in order to buy one specific item (i.e. a washing machine)

- *SSI (Supplemental Security Income)* Governmental payments made to low-income, disabled individuals.

- *Windfalls* Unexpected money.

- *Working Savings* A savings account into which you contribute regularly and out of which you pay extraordinary bills

LINDA BESSETTE *(r.)*, a graduate of Rhode Island College with sixteen years' experience in business finance, has counseled individuals and small businesses in money management for many years. ANNE OWINGS WILSON *(l.)* has practiced law for fourteen years and serves on the faculty of the University of Arkansas for Medical Sciences, where she teaches a course on women and health care. Both authors live in Little Rock, Arkansas, where they maintain private practices. HELEN T. BENNET *(not pictured)* received her Ph.D. from Brown University and is an Associate Professor of English at Eastern Kentucky University.